Ring of Power

Role of Reserve Currency in Rise and Fall of Empires

Dr. Tirdad Aryan

Publisher: Stone Ridge Press

Title: *Ring of Power: Role of Reserve Currency in Rise and Fall of Empires*

Author: Tirdad Aryan

ISBN: 978-1-968554-01-9

Format: Trade Paperback

Product Series: Kush

First Edition: June 2025

A Word from the Publisher

At Stone Ridge, we believe everyone shares the responsibility to make the world a better place. Kindness and knowledge are alike—they grow when shared. For every print copy of this book sold, we donate a dollar to the charity below. Help us by following, sharing, and recommending our books.

Proceeds from this book will go to:

**St. Jude Children's®
Research Hospital**
Finding cures. Saving children.
ALSAC · DANNY THOMAS, FOUNDER

If you want to contribute as an author and publish your work with us, please visit stoneridgepress.org or contact us at info@stoneridgepress.org.

Dedicated to the love of my life and my parents.

Dr. Tirdad Aryan

tirdad.aryan@blockhousefinancial.com

A blacksmith lived with his wife and only son.

The blacksmith's son was lazy and spent most of his time playing and having fun in the streets.

Years passed, and the blacksmith became old and sick. He could no longer work. His son was also idle and did not help him.

One night, the blacksmith turned to his son and said, "I have worked hard for years so that you and your mother could live comfortably. Now that I am old and sick and unable to work, it is your responsibility to work and take care of the family."

The son was upset. He didn't want to work at all. The next morning, the son went out to find work. The blacksmith's wife, who loved her son dearly, gave him some coins and said, "When you return home tonight, you can give these to your father and tell him that it is your payment for the day's work."

The son happily left the house and hung out with his friends until sunset. He returned home tired and gave the coins to the blacksmith. The blacksmith threw the coins into the fire, "You didn't earn this money. You should stop being lazy and go find a real job," he said.

The next day, the blacksmith's wife gave the son more coins. In the evening, the son returned home and handed the coins to the blacksmith, who looked at it and threw it into the fire again.

The son was surprised by his father's actions, but he didn't protest. The father said, "Son, you didn't earn these coins either. You need to stop being lazy and go find a job."

On the third day, the same thing happened again.

On the fourth day, the blacksmith's wife told her son, "This isn't working. Your father will understand. It's better if you find a job for yourself."

The son went to the market and started working in a shoemaker's shop. At sunset, he received some coins and returned home tired. He handed the coins to his father, who stared at it for a while before throwing it into the fire. Without hesitation, the son rushed to the fireplace and began digging through the burning logs with his bare hands.

He pulled them out quickly, brushing off the ash, and turned back to his father with fury in his eyes, ready to protest.

The father smiled and said, "Well done, son. This is what you earned!"

Contents

Chapter 1

Echoes of Power

At the heart of every empire lies a paradox: the very power that lifts a nation to global dominance can, if left unchecked, bring about its unraveling. Nowhere is this more evident than in the story of reserve currencies. From Rome to Britain to the present day, the lesson is always the same—currency hegemony is a double-edged sword. It tempts a nation with its promises of limitless consumption, unrivaled financial influence, and effortless power. But over time, that same privilege hollows out the foundations of economic reality, transforming vibrant production into complacent consumption, turning industrious citizens into entitled dependents, and concentrating both wealth and policy into fewer, more unaccountable hands. What begins as a tool of strength becomes a trap of illusion. The allure of being the world's reserve currency is rooted in the power it gives: the power to print what others must earn, the power to dictate global financial terms, the power to fund wars and welfare alike without the immediate cost of taxation. But that power is not free. It imposes a toll on the issuing nation, a slow decay of discipline, competitiveness, and realism. As the issuer gains financial dominance, it loses the habits that made it great. It sacrifices its manufacturing, its savings, its technological edge, and ultimately its social fabric. The world sees it as strong, even as it rots from within.

There is something seductive about the idea of a nation becoming the financial center of the globe. Capital flows in. Talent comes knocking. The stock market soars. Property prices rise. Consumption becomes effortless. Imports are paid for not with goods or innovation, but with newly printed money. And yet, under the surface, everything that matters begins to slip away. The machinery that builds, the education that innovates, the character that sacrifices—these fade. Financial services thrive not because they support a strong real economy, but because they replace it. Politics is no longer about vision or national purpose—it becomes about how to distribute the ever-growing monetary spoils, or how to conceal the declining real economy behind rising financial metrics. Over time, the reserve currency issuer begins to rule not by merit but by inertia. It maintains its position not because it is still the strongest producer or innovator, but because it still controls the pipes through which global money flows. This is where resentment begins to brew. Other nations, even allies, begin to see the system as unfair. They question why one country is allowed to run permanent deficits while they must struggle to maintain fiscal discipline.

They ask why their savings must be invested in assets denominated in another nation's currency, exposed to the whims of its central bank and political class. They wonder how long they must play a game rigged by historical accident.

Chapter 2

Doom of Dominion

In the ancient world, the idea of a dominant medium of exchange was tied closely to physical commodities like gold and silver. But even among these, certain coins and monetary systems gained trust and usage far beyond their origin points. The earliest known example of such monetary dominance was during the reign of ancient Athens. During the 5th century BCE, the silver drachma of Athens became widely accepted across the Mediterranean world. This was due to the economic and military dominance of Athens in the Delian League, as well as the trusted quality of the silver mined at Laurium. As Athenian trade expanded, so did the acceptance of its coinage. The drachma was simple, recognizable, and considered trustworthy. However, the rise of Sparta, the Peloponnesian War, and eventual Macedonian conquest weakened Athenian power. The drachma lost its global significance, not due to hyperinflation or monetary mismanagement, but because the military and political center of gravity shifted.

In the centuries that followed, the Macedonian and then Roman Empires established monetary dominance. The Roman denarius emerged as the primary currency of trade across a vast territory from Britain to Egypt. Rome's dominance in trade, infrastructure, and administration gave its coinage a credibility no rival could match. For centuries, the silver denarius and later the gold aureus and solidus served as the most reliable store of value and medium of exchange. But Rome's decline brought about one of the earliest and most dramatic cases of monetary collapse. By the 3rd century CE, the Roman Empire began debasing its currency to fund military expenditures and administrative costs. The silver content of the denarius plummeted. What began as a slow erosion of trust culminated in full-scale hyperinflation during the Crisis of the Third Century. The empire fractured, trade collapsed, and a barter economy returned in many regions. The trust in Roman coinage, once the pillar of economic order, was shattered. The Diocletian reforms tried to stabilize the situation, and Constantine's introduction of the solidus in the 4th century helped reestablish some monetary stability. The solidus, a high-purity gold coin, continued to be minted in the Eastern Roman (Byzantine) Empire and circulated across Europe and the Middle East for centuries. It was remarkably stable and served as a de facto reserve currency in many parts of the world.

However, as the Byzantine Empire weakened, and the Islamic Caliphates rose, a new currency began to dominate. The

Islamic dinar and dirham, introduced during the Umayyad Caliphate in the 7th century, became trusted forms of money from the Iberian Peninsula to Central Asia. The stability of the Islamic world, especially during the Abbasid Golden Age, the extensive trade networks, and the uniformity of Islamic law which regulated coinage and prevented arbitrary debasement, made these coins desirable. The gold dinar, in particular, became a reference currency in Europe during the early medieval period. But like others before it, the dominance of Islamic currencies waned as the Caliphates fragmented, and European powers slowly began to rise. The next major shift came with the rise of the Italian city-states during the late Middle Ages. Chief among these was Venice. The Venetian gold ducat, introduced in the 13th century, gained wide acceptance in Mediterranean trade and beyond. Venice's reputation for stability, maritime trade dominance, and its ability to maintain the purity of its coinage ensured the ducat's prominence for over five hundred years. It was often imitated by other states and was trusted by merchants from North Africa to Northern Europe.

As Venice declined, the power center shifted again. The rise of the Portuguese and Spanish empires in the 15th and 16th centuries, driven by exploration and colonization, brought about new monetary centers. Spain, in particular, ushered in an era of vast silver flows from the Americas into Europe and Asia. The Spanish "piece of eight" (the silver peso) became the world's most widely used coin in the early modern period. It circulated across Europe, the Americas, and

Asia—especially in China, which used silver as the backbone of its monetary system. The Spanish dollar effectively became the first global currency, the result of imperial reach, mercantilist policy, and the sheer volume of silver mined from the New World. However, this dependence on precious metals proved unstable. By the 17th century, the sheer influx of silver into Europe, combined with inefficient taxation and war spending, began to cause inflation. Spain, burdened with constant wars and administrative bloat, suffered a series of sovereign defaults—five between 1557 and 1653. These defaults eroded trust in the Spanish monarchy's financial competence. While the coinage itself retained its silver content, the broader trust in Spain's economic management and its weakening global dominance contributed to the gradual decline of the Spanish dollar's central role.

By the late 1600s, the Dutch Republic emerged as a new financial power. The guilder, backed by the credibility of the Amsterdam Wisselbank (a precursor to the modern central bank), became the currency of choice in Europe. More than the coin itself, it was the banking and financial infrastructure of the Dutch that inspired trust. The guilder's rise marked a turning point in reserve currency history—from purely metallic standards to systems backed by institutional strength. Amsterdam became the center of international finance. Bills of exchange, letters of credit, and early forms of government bonds all played roles in consolidating the guilder's influence. Still, the Dutch Republic was small and vulnerable. Its power, while significant in finance, could not be maintained in the face of rising military competitors like France and England. As the 18th century unfolded, Britain's victory in key global conflicts—particularly the Seven Years' War—signaled a new phase. The British Empire gained control over vast territories, including India and large parts of North America. Its navy ruled the seas, and its economic strength grew.

The British pound sterling, backed by the strength of the Bank of England and the gold standard, became the new reserve currency of the world. The Industrial Revolution, centered in Britain, gave further momentum to the pound. London became the world's financial capital. The British Empire's dominance in trade, colonial governance, and naval power ensured that the pound sterling was used for settling debts, financing trade, and holding reserves. The 19th century is often regarded as the era of the British pound—the first true modern reserve currency backed by institutional credibility, gold convertibility, and global influence. However, even the pound sterling's dominance was not eternal. The seeds of its decline were sown in the 20th century, particularly during the First World War. Britain's massive war expenditures led to a suspension of the gold standard and significant borrowing. The interwar years were characterized by repeated efforts to return to prewar parity, but these efforts were undermined by global instability, economic depression, and Britain's relative decline in industrial output compared to the United States and Germany.

While the German Deutsche Mark never rose to the level

of global dominance achieved by the British pound or the U.S. dollar, it did function as a significant secondary reserve currency during the latter half of the 20th century. The Deutsche Mark traces its origins to the economic chaos following World War I. At the time, Germany used the Papiermark, a fiat currency issued in large quantities to finance war expenses. After Germany's defeat in 1918, the country was saddled with enormous reparations under the Treaty of Versailles. With little gold or hard assets left, and no access to foreign borrowing, the Weimar government resorted to printing more money to cover its obligations. This marked the beginning of one of the most extreme hyperinflation episodes in recorded history.

By 1921, inflation was already destabilizing the German economy, but in 1923, it spiraled out of control. Prices doubled every few days, then every few hours. At the height of the crisis, the exchange rate plummeted from 4.2 marks per U.S. dollar in 1914 to 4.2 trillion marks per dollar by November 1923. The cost of basic goods became astronomical, wages were rendered meaningless, and people carried baskets of money just to buy bread. Entire classes of savers were wiped out, and economic uncertainty fed political extremism, setting the stage for the social unrest of the 1930s and the rise of radical ideologies. To end the crisis, the German government introduced a new currency in late 1923, the Rentenmark, backed by land and industrial assets rather than gold. This stabilized the economy temporarily and was later replaced by the Reichsmark, which lasted until the end of World War II. However, by 1948, with Germany again in ruins and under Allied occupation, the Reichsmark had become nearly worthless due to wartime destruction, black-market distortions, and widespread economic dysfunction. In response, the U.S., Britain, and France coordinated a currency reform in West Germany, replacing the Reichsmark with the Deutsche Mark.

Britain attempted to return to the gold standard in 1925 at its prewar parity, a move encouraged by traditionalists who believed in the symbolic strength of the pound. But this overvalued the currency relative to the weakened postwar British economy, causing exports to stagnate, unemployment to rise, and deflationary pressures to build. By 1931, under intense economic and political strain, Britain finally abandoned the gold standard. This marked the end of the pound's uncontested role as the world's reserve currency. Meanwhile, across the Atlantic, the United States was emerging as the world's foremost industrial and financial power. Although the U.S. had maintained a relatively isolationist posture during much of the 19th century, its economy had grown explosively through industrialization, infrastructure development, and a vast internal market. The First World War saw the U.S. become the largest creditor nation, replacing Britain as the global financial backstop. The situation worsened in the 1930s, as countries engaged in competitive devaluations and protectionism. Britain formally abandoned the gold standard in 1931. Although the pound still retained some international significance, its role as a stable reserve currency was weakened. By the time World War II broke out, it was clear that the pound could no longer serve as the central pillar of the international monetary system. As the British Empire entered the 20th century, its global influence was still vast, but signs of decline had become apparent. The First World War exposed the limits of Britain's economic and military power. Financing the war had required enormous borrowing, particularly from the United States, and had forced Britain off the gold standard.

The Great Depression in the 1930s momentarily destabilized this trajectory. In 1933, President Franklin D. Roosevelt suspended the dollar's convertibility into gold for domestic transactions and later devalued the dollar relative to gold, ending the long-standing \$20.67/oz rate and resetting it to \$35/oz. Yet even during this period of economic turmoil, the U.S. dollar retained a relative strength. It was backed by the world's largest gold reserves and a still-functioning industrial economy. Foreign governments and institutions began increasingly holding dollars as a hedge, even as confidence in other currencies waned. World War II marked the definitive geopolitical and economic shift from Britain to the United States. The war devastated Europe and Asia, destroyed infrastructure, crippled industries, and forced nations to rely heavily on American loans, weapons, and supplies. The U.S., in contrast, experienced a wartime economic boom. It became the "arsenal of democracy," and by 1945, held more than two-thirds of the world's gold reserves and nearly half of global industrial output. The dollar had become de facto indispensable—not just for war financing but for rebuilding the global order.

Chapter 3

Bretton Woods

By the end of the Second World War, it became clear that the old system of competitive currencies, gold parity confusion, and fragmented trade regimes needed replacement. The war had exposed the vulnerabilities of national economies and the destructive nature of unchecked monetary chaos. In response, 44 Allied nations gathered in July 1944 at Bretton Woods, New Hampshire, to design a new international monetary order. This gathering produced the Bretton Woods Agreement, which sought to stabilize global finance and rebuild economies through structured cooperation. The Bretton Woods system was revolutionary in its ambitions but pragmatic in design. It proposed a fixed exchange rate regime where all participating currencies were pegged to the U.S. dollar, and the dollar itself was pegged to gold at a fixed rate of $35 per ounce. This gave the dollar a unique role as the anchor of the international financial system, effectively replacing the British pound. It was not only the dollar's gold backing that inspired confidence but also the unparalleled economic strength of the United States, its industrial base, and political institutions. The Bretton Woods framework introduced international institutions to monitor and support global finance. The International Monetary Fund (IMF) was created to provide short-term assistance to countries with balance-of-payment issues and to oversee exchange rate policies. The World Bank was established to facilitate long-term reconstruction and development, especially in war-torn regions. These institutions were headquartered in Washington, D.C., underscoring the central role of the United States in postwar economic leadership. What truly solidified the dollar's dominance was not only its link to gold but also the strength and credibility of U.S. institutions. The Federal Reserve, though imperfect, was relatively independent and capable of managing monetary policy without succumbing to short-term political pressures. The U.S. economy was open, capital markets were deep and liquid, and the political system was stable. These features made the dollar attractive for global trade and for central banks holding foreign reserves.

Despite its strengths, the Bretton Woods system contained a core weakness: the need for the United States to supply the world with dollars to facilitate global trade, while simultaneously guaranteeing that those dollars could be converted into gold. This contradiction, known as the Triffin Dilemma, became increasingly apparent during the 1960s. As the U.S. increased spending on Cold War engagements, especially the Vietnam War, and expanded domestic welfare programs, it began running persistent trade and budget deficits. Meanwhile, Europe and Japan had recovered economically, and they began to accumulate significant dollar reserves. By the late 1960s, global confidence in the dollar's gold convertibility began to erode. Nations such as France, under President Charles de Gaulle, began demanding gold in exchange for their dollar holdings. Speculation mounted, and pressure on U.S. gold reserves intensified. The tipping point came in August 1971, when President Richard Nixon suspended the convertibility of the dollar into gold, effectively ending the Bretton Woods system.

The decision to suspend dollar convertibility into gold marked the transition from a gold-backed monetary system to a fiat currency regime, where the value of money is based on collective trust rather than tangible assets. Surprisingly, the dollar did not collapse. Instead, it adapted and endured. With the United States holding unmatched military power and economic dominance, other nations had little practical alternative. Most lacked the means to challenge the U.S. financially or militarily, and amid global uncertainty, it was better to have something stable—even if imperfect—than nothing at all. The U.S. economy, supported by its vast industrial capacity, technological innovation, and geopolitical influence, continued to command global confidence. As a result, the dollar remained the most widely held and traded currency, solidifying its role as the world's primary reserve asset—a status it maintains in the floating exchange rate system that shapes global finance to this day.

Chapter 4

Soul of Money

In economics, intrinsic value refers to the actual value of an asset, independent of market perception or speculation. For a currency, this value can come from two main sources. First, it may be tied to something with universally accepted worth—such as gold, oil, or other commodities. Second, it may be backed by the economic productivity of a nation and be easily convertible into financial assets like stocks, bonds, or real estate. In both cases, the currency can be exchanged for things that have real-world utility or yield returns. A reserve currency must offer this intrinsic value because nations do not hold currency for its own sake. Exporting countries earn reserves to use them later—either to import goods, invest in foreign markets, stabilize their own currencies, or build financial cushions in times of economic stress. Without intrinsic value or convertibility, holding a currency becomes an act of speculation rather than a strategic financial choice.

Bitcoin, despite its innovative technology and growing popularity in speculative markets, lacks intrinsic value in the way required for a stable reserve currency. It is not backed by physical goods, a productive economy, or any issuing state. In the global economy, it's not enough for a currency to be spendable—it must be part of a broader system of trust, value preservation, and reciprocal obligations. Unlike in fiat systems, nothing binds the importer to reacquire or maintain Bitcoin holdings. There's no institutional structure or economic policy ensuring that Bitcoin returns to circulation through symmetric trade. In contrast, fiat-based reserve currencies like the U.S. dollar are embedded in a network of mutual dependencies, central bank reserves, and trade obligations that keep the currency in circulation and highly liquid. Exporters such as China, Germany, or Saudi Arabia accept dollars not only because they can be used to import goods, but because those dollars can be reinvested in U.S. Treasury bonds, global financial markets, and multinational corporations. They yield interest, preserve capital, and can be safely stored in vast quantities.

Bitcoin offers none of these features. It provides no yield, no credit structure, no institutional backing. If the world were to switch to Bitcoin as the global reserve currency overnight, this cycle would disintegrate. Exporting nations would receive a digital asset that cannot earn interest, cannot easily be converted into tangible financial products, and may fluctuate wildly in value. And what if a country accumulates a large Bitcoin reserve—let's say China or Saudi Arabia ends up holding a significant share of global Bitcoin supply. What strategic advantage does this bring? Unlike dollars, which can be recycled into American debt, multinational assets, or global commodity purchases, Bitcoin offers no investment infrastructure. It doesn't create a cycle of global reinvestment—it just sits. Worse, if the country decides to liquidate a portion of its holdings, the impact on Bitcoin's price could be catastrophic. The act of selling itself could cause depreciation, which makes large holdings in Bitcoin a fragile asset rather than a strategic one.

In a currency without intrinsic value—one not backed by a state, a productive economy, or real financial assets—the larger your share of it, the more exposed you become to systemic risk. Unlike fiat reserve currencies such as the U.S. dollar, where central banks and global institutions have a vested interest in maintaining stability, non-intrinsic currencies like Bitcoin lack collective defense mechanisms. No country is obligated to preserve its value or ensure liquidity. In fact, the more Bitcoin a country accumulates, the greater its vulnerability to market shifts caused by others exiting the system. Since there is no underlying obligation or institutional trust tying other participants to the currency, a country with large holdings finds itself hostage to volatility it cannot control and incentives it cannot align. This creates a dangerous asymmetry. In traditional systems, widespread adoption of a reserve currency increases its resilience, as stakeholders have incentives to maintain its credibility and demand. But with a non-intrinsic value currency, adoption does not equate to commitment. Other countries can easily opt out, shift to alternative assets, or convert to a more stable medium without institutional penalty. The more dominant your position, the more exposed you are to price collapse and liquidity crises, especially when others are not economically or politically bound to defend the system you've invested in.

To understand why the U.S. dollar remains the world's dominant reserve currency, one must look beyond America's military or political influence. The real reason is trust—trust not only in the U.S. government but in its economic and financial systems. The dollar is supported by the world's largest economy, a deep and liquid financial market, a transparent legal system, and a central bank with a long record of managing crises. U.S. Treasury bonds, denominated in dollars, are among the most reliable financial instruments globally. Countries accumulate dollars because they can be quickly and safely converted into these assets, which provide stable returns and can be sold with minimal risk. Even after the gold standard was abandoned in the 1970s, the dollar's dominance continued due to the strength of American financial institutions. Nations still chose to hold dollars because the U.S. offered a functioning, open economy where money could be safely parked and reliably accessed.

Another key point in understanding the stability of the dollar as the global reserve currency is the concept of mutually assured economic destruction. The United States issues dollar-denominated debt on a massive scale, and a significant portion of this debt is held by foreign governments, financial institutions, and central banks. If the U.S. were to default on its obligations or allow the dollar to collapse in value, it would not only devastate global markets but also wreak havoc on its own financial system. The ripple effects would severely damage U.S. creditworthiness, raise borrowing costs, devalue domestic savings, and destabilize the broader economy. In essence, the U.S. has a vested interest in maintaining the dollar's credibility—because undermining it would directly threaten its own economic survival. This self-reinforcing mechanism generates a strong incentive to uphold the dollar's value, making it a trustworthy vehicle for global trade and reserves.

A basket of currencies, while often proposed as a more balanced and neutral alternative to a single-nation reserve currency, introduces a host of complications that undermine its practicality and long-term viability. A basket system, composed of multiple currencies like the euro, yen, yuan, and dollar, would require managing reserves across various national financial systems, each with different regulatory environments, interest rates, political risks, and capital controls. This fragmentation not only reduces efficiency but also increases risk, as shocks in one currency or country can affect the value of the entire basket. Investors and central banks would need to continuously rebalance their holdings, creating complex hedging requirements and introducing currency risk at a systemic level. Beyond reinvestment, a basket of currencies creates unresolved issues around responsibility and coordination. Who manages the basket? Who responds in a

crisis? Unlike a single sovereign issuer—such as the U.S. in
the case of the dollar—no single country in a currency basket
is accountable for maintaining the basket's overall stability.
Each nation has its own monetary policy priorities, interest
rate targets, and inflation controls. These may conflict with
the collective stability required of a reserve system. For example, if Japan pursues aggressive monetary easing while the
eurozone tightens its policy, the relative weights and effects
on the basket fluctuate in unpredictable ways. No central
authority has the mandate or legitimacy to coordinate these
policies for the benefit of global stability. In such a setup,
the reserve currency becomes a moving target, undermining
its role as a predictable and trusted store of value.

Some argue that countries could simply agree to use a new
reserve currency, whether it's a digital yuan, a euro-backed
basket, or a central bank digital currency. In theory, this
is possible. But in practice, reaching global consensus is
immensely difficult. Trust must be earned, not declared.
Even the euro, used by twenty-plus countries with a combined GDP rivaling that of the U.S., has not displaced the
dollar. This is due to structural issues within the EU, incon-
sistent fiscal policies, and political fragmentation. A new reserve currency would require more than agreement—it would
require a credible economic foundation, the ability to offer
financial instruments that are safe and liquid, and a governance model that assures the world the system won't collapse
under stress. The reserve currency of the world is not chosen
at random, nor can it be imposed by ideology or technology

alone. It must emerge from economic realities and be supported by real incentives. Intrinsic value—whether through direct worth or convertibility into financial assets—is at the core of this system. Exporters need to be compensated with something that has utility, stability, and return. Investors need instruments that are safe and liquid. Central banks need assets they can trust in times of crisis. Until there is a credible alternative with real-world value, financial convertibility, and the architecture of trust behind it, the world will continue to rely on the dollar.

Chapter 5

Master of Coins

The state that commands the dominant reserve currency enjoys an unrivaled advantage in global affairs. This monetary supremacy allows it to print the very currency in which most global debts are denominated, to finance fiscal deficits without the punitive constraints faced by other nations, and to exert control over global trade and capital flows. Unsurprisingly, a state that wields such power will go to great lengths to prevent the rise of any competing currency that might threaten its privileged position. This reality explains the persistent absence of any serious contender to the reigning global reserve currency and why, in such a manipulated landscape, the only viable alternative has always been—and perhaps always will be—gold.

The concept of a reserve currency appears straightforward, it is the currency held in large quantities by foreign governments and institutions as a store of value and medium for international transactions. When a currency is globally adopted as a reserve, its issuing country gains significant leverage over international trade, capital flows, and economic diplomacy. More importantly, it begins to shape the rules of the global financial system. In such a dynamic, the emergence of an alternative reserve currency is not merely an economic development—it signals the birth of a rival power center. Broad acceptance of a new reserve currency would mark the rise of a state or bloc capable of commanding global confidence, asserting financial independence, and offering an alternative to existing systems of control. This development would not only weaken the existing hegemon's capacity to influence the world through economic mechanisms, but it would also embolden the new issuer to challenge norms, project its values abroad, and build parallel institutions that bypass established ones.

The risk lies not just in economic competition, but in the strategic consequences of yielding such influence. A newly empowered currency issuer could restrict access to capital markets, impose its own regulatory standards, and weaponize its monetary tools just as previous hegemons have done. Even more dangerously, it could erode existing alliances by offering more flexible or less politically conditioned financial alternatives to developing nations and smaller states, thereby redrawing spheres of influence without firing a shot. To avoid ceding this kind of strategic ground, the current hegemon acts decisively to prevent any other currency to serve as reserve except its own. It does so not out of economic self-interest alone, but from a recognition that allowing another country to ascend as the issuer of a widely held reserve currency poses an existential threat to its own dominance. Attempts by the European Union to elevate the euro to reserve status have repeatedly run into political roadblocks and crises that, while sometimes self-inflicted, have also been amplified by narratives and actions that subtly undermine its credibility. Similarly, China's renminbi, despite the country's economic weight, remains shackled by capital controls, geopolitical suspicion, and institutional inertia—all of which serve to protect the primacy of the dollar. In this environment, where all fiat alternatives are suppressed or inherently flawed due to dependence on centralized political systems, gold stands out as the only neutral, apolitical, and historical alternative. Unlike fiat currencies, gold is not issued by any state and does not require trust in a particular government or central bank. It is immune to printing presses, geopolitical sanctions, and policy missteps.

Gold's role as money is as old as civilization itself. From ancient Mesopotamia to the Roman Empire, from the Byzantine solidus to the gold dinar and florin, gold has consistently been chosen across time and geography as a medium of exchange, a store of value, and a unit of account. This near-universal preference is not coincidental. Gold possesses unique physical and chemical properties that make it exceptionally suited for monetary use. It is scarce but not too scarce, malleable enough for coinage and bullion, non-corrosive and durable enough to last centuries without degradation. Unlike commodities like oil or wheat, gold is not consumed or destroyed through use, which means virtually all the gold ever mined still exists in some form, creating a stable supply that grows only marginally each year. This slow and predictable rate of supply expansion mirrors the kind of monetary stability that fiat currencies often aspire to but rarely achieve. Furthermore, gold is uniquely resistant to centralization. While governments may own significant reserves, no single state can control its production or manipulate its issuance. It cannot be printed at will or conjured out of political necessity. This makes it an ideal counterweight to the discretionary power of central banks and an anchor of trust in times of monetary uncertainty. Historically, when fiat regimes collapsed or hyperinflation took hold—as in Weimar Germany, Zimbabwe, or more recently Venezuela—people inevitably reverted to gold or gold-linked stores of value as a means of preserving purchasing power.

The last century saw an experiment with a hybrid model of fiat-gold backing through the Bretton Woods system. Under this system, the U.S. dollar was convertible to gold at a fixed rate, effectively making it a global currency backed by gold. This arrangement gave the appearance of dollar hegemony while retaining the confidence of gold's convertibility. However, the system proved unsustainable. As the United States printed more dollars than it could back with its gold reserves, foreign governments—most notably France—began demanding physical gold in exchange for their dollar holdings. In 1971, the U.S. unilaterally ended convertibility, severing the last tie between fiat currency and gold and inaugurating the era of fully unbacked money. Since then, the dollar has retained its reserve currency status not through intrinsic value but through institutional dominance: control of international financial infrastructure, military supremacy, and global trust in the U.S. economy. However, these foundations are not immutable. As geopolitical tensions rise and fiscal deficits balloon, the risks associated with excessive reliance on a single fiat currency are becoming more evident. Central banks around the world have begun to quietly increase their gold holdings, not because of nostalgia, but because of strategic foresight. Gold is the only asset that is no one's liability, a characteristic that makes it uniquely suited for reserves in a world where trust is increasingly scarce.

Unlike currencies tied to the policies of governments, gold has no political allegiance. It is the ultimate bearer asset, requiring no intermediaries or counterparties. In a multipolar world with fragmented alliances, digital surveillance, and rising sovereign risk, these features are becoming invaluable. Gold can be transported, verified, and transacted without reliance on the infrastructure of the hegemon. It can serve as collateral, settlement medium, and hedge—all without the risk of asset freezes, inflationary dilution, or capital controls. To be sure, gold is not without limitations. It is not easily divisible for everyday transactions, and its lack of yield makes it less attractive in times of monetary stability and economic growth. However, these are logistical challenges, not fundamental flaws. Technological innovations such as digital gold certificates, blockchain-based tokenization, and distributed storage networks are increasingly bridging the gap between gold's physical nature and the requirements of a modern financial system. The goal is not necessarily to replace fiat currencies with gold, but to restore gold's role as a parallel reserve asset—a neutral benchmark of value that disciplines monetary excess and anchors trust.

Chapter 6

Burdens of Bullion

No matter how hard I tried to sell you on the merits of gold as the reserve currency, beneath its lustrous surface, it carries fundamental constraints that render it ill-suited to underpin twenty-first-century global finance. A careful analysis reveals that the physical nature of gold, its scale limitations, the absence of a fiat-clearing mechanism, the trust placed in its custodians, and the military-backing implicitly required to secure it all conspire to make gold an unwieldy choice in an era of instantaneous electronic commerce and complex sovereign interdependence. Gold's physicality imposes friction on an economy that increasingly depends on the virtual transfer of value. Modern trade flows rest on digital messaging networks that settle obligations in an instant, without the need to exchange anything tangible. By contrast, gold demands transport, storage, verification and insurance at every stage of settlement. If a central bank in Singapore owes another in São Paulo, gold bars cannot be beamed across fiber-optic cables; they must be crated, guarded and ferried on armored vehicles or loaded onto planes. Each transfer incurs cost, risk and delay—factors largely absent when account balances simply update in a ledger. As trade volumes have mushroomed over the past decades, these logistical burdens would scale linearly or worse, rather than diminishing through digital efficiencies. The resulting drag on liquidity and the higher transaction costs would force counterparties to erect additional buffers of gold reserves, further throttling the velocity of money and exacerbating the very scarcity that promoters of a gold standard decry.

The notion of fiat money pegged to gold, as once practiced by many nations, suffers from its own peril: it places enormous trust in the "guardian" that holds and manages the reserve. Under such systems, paper currency becomes nothing more than a promise of convertibility on demand. History teaches us that these promises can be—and have been—broken. In August 1971, President Nixon suspended the convertibility of U.S. dollars into gold, effectively nullifying the Bretton Woods arrangement and exposing the fragility of gold-pegged fiats. That decision was driven by a confluence of war-financing pressures, balance-of-payments deficits and the overhang of dollar liabilities held abroad. When the trust placed in America's ability to redeem dollars for gold evaporated, it unleashed a cascade of currency realignments and ushered in the current era of floating exchange rates. This rupture highlights that any gold-pegged fiat must rest on the credibility and discretion of its issuing authority—an inherently political and potentially unstable foundation.

Further complicating matters is the fact that any truly intrinsic value currency demands a guardian with sufficient coercive power to protect it against theft or expropriation. Gold, unlike digital ledger entries, can be stolen by clandestine operations or grand larceny. Entire national reserves have been lost to wartime looting, covert raids, or plainclothes schemes of asset misappropriation. To safeguard vast hoards of bullion, a state must commit substantial resources to naval fleets, air patrols, secure vaults, and counterintelligence—an implicit subsidy in its defense budget. Those expenses, in turn, place further strain on government finances and carry the risk of militarizing monetary policy. In contrast, modern fiat monies circulate as intangible credits, largely immune from physical plunder. They rely instead on cyber-security, legal agreements, and interbank guarantees—all of which benefit from networked systems rather than solitary stockpiles vulnerable to brute force.

Pegging the global monetary standard to the output or reserves of any single country, even one as large as the United States, would inextricably entangle international finance with that nation's fiscal and monetary policy choices. When a country issues its own currency, it calibrates the money supply, interest rates and budget deficits according to domestic priorities. If the entire world demanded U.S. dollars redeemable in gold, every expansion of U.S. fiscal spending or quantitative easing program would ripple across borders, forcing foreign central banks to accumulate or shed dollar reserves in lockstep. Similarly, U.S. decisions to tighten credit or shrink its gold stockpile would induce global deflationary pressures. Such externalities run counter to the principle that sovereign economic policies should not bayonet international stability. A truly global standard must therefore transcend any one political jurisdiction, maintaining insulation between national agendas and the broader need for financial equilibrium.

Taken together, these dimensions—physical transport and storage costs, limited global supplies, absence of an elastic fiat clearing system, reliance on fallible custodial promises, the need for military-grade protection, and the impossibility of divorcing one nation's fiscal policy from global money—make gold a problematic cornerstone for twenty-first-century reserves. While gold will undoubtedly continue to serve as a portfolio diversifier, a hedge against inflation, or a symbol of monetary steadiness, it cannot readily shoulder the dynamic demands of modern trade, finance and developmental policy. Instead, the world has gravitated toward fiat currencies backed by the collective faith of governments and governed by institutional frameworks capable of swift adjustment. These systems leverage technology, legal infrastructures and multilateral cooperation—tools that a purely gold-based regime lacks. In that light, the dream of a renewed gold standard appears less a return to monetary virtue than a retreat into constraints that today's economies cannot afford.

Chapter 7

Allure

In the architecture of international power, few instruments offer as silent and enduring an advantage as holding the status of the world's reserve currency. For a hegemon, the temptation to install its own currency in this privileged position stems not just from economic convenience, but from the extraordinary range of influence it unlocks across trade, finance, security, and diplomacy. Being the issuer of the dominant reserve currency creates a structural asymmetry in the global system—an asymmetry that rewards the hegemon with benefits that reach far beyond what any other nation can claim, and with tools that allow it to shape the global order on its own terms. A reserve currency is, by definition, the currency that is widely used by other countries as a medium of exchange, store of value, and unit of account in international trade and finance. Central banks hold it as a significant portion of their foreign exchange reserves; international loans and commodity contracts are often denominated in it; and cross-border investments tend to be conducted through its channels.

This widespread usage generates a persistent global demand for the currency, which becomes embedded in the infrastructure of the global economy—its contracts, its banking systems, and its pricing models. This demand has profound consequences. For the hegemon, it means that the rest of the world must accumulate its currency, usually by running trade surpluses with it or investing in its debt instruments. As a result, the hegemon can effectively export its currency in exchange for real goods and services, incurring trade deficits with little immediate consequence. The currency it prints is not simply consumed domestically—it becomes the oil that lubricates the machinery of global commerce. This dynamic allows the hegemon to run fiscal and trade deficits without the destabilizing effects that such imbalances would provoke in other economies. Unlike other nations, it is not required to produce a balanced inflow of foreign currency before it can spend abroad. It can simply issue liabilities in its own money, confident that global actors will accept and hold them.

Beyond trade, the role of reserve currency issuer provides unmatched advantages in sovereign finance. The hegemon enjoys what economists call "seigniorage"—the ability to create money at a cost near zero and exchange it for goods, services, or productive assets globally. This privilege is most visible in times of crisis. While other countries must raise interest rates to defend their currencies or secure access to foreign capital, the hegemon often experiences the opposite:

capital flows in during global instability, as investors seek the safety of the reserve currency. The hegemon's bonds are not only a source of financing but are seen as the ultimate collateral in the global financial system. Its central bank becomes a lender of last resort not just for domestic institutions but for foreign governments, multinational banks, and entire regions. With the world transacting and saving in its currency, the hegemon gains a unique form of leverage—one that allows it to shape the rules of global finance and exert influence far beyond its borders. This influence manifests in the form of control over payment systems, access to capital markets, and regulatory standards. For example, when the hegemon imposes financial sanctions, they carry global weight because international transactions often require the use of its currency and, by extension, its financial infrastructure. Even companies and countries with no direct exposure to the hegemon's domestic market may find themselves subject to its regulations simply because they must pass through its currency networks.

Furthermore, the hegemon's monetary policy decisions reverberate across the world. When it lowers interest rates, capital often floods into emerging markets, fueling credit booms; when it tightens, that capital retreats, creating volatility. In this way, the hegemon can indirectly shape global growth cycles, influence the borrowing costs of other nations, and exercise a quiet yet formidable authority over the economic trajectories of others. No direct decree is needed—its influence is exercised through liquidity, pricing, and expectations. At home, reserve currency status transforms the financial landscape. It supports lower interest rates by ensuring strong demand for government debt, enabling expansive fiscal policy with relatively mild inflationary consequences. It boosts the financial sector by increasing the global usage of domestic banks, payment systems, and investment firms. It enhances the attractiveness of domestic capital markets, drawing foreign investment into equities, real estate, and startups. As the rest of the world holds the hegemon's liabilities as reserves, those reserves are typically reinvested in its assets, creating a positive feedback loop that boosts domestic liquidity and asset prices.

When a country's currency becomes the world's reserve, it gains an aura of credibility and permanence. It is seen as a symbol of stability, competence, and dominance. This symbolism, while abstract, has very real consequences. It reinforces investor confidence, sustains the hegemony of its institutions, and supports the global adoption of its economic model. It also elevates its status in diplomatic negotiations, international summits, and multilateral forums. A nation whose currency is the basis of global commerce speaks with greater authority and is listened to with closer attention. But perhaps most seductively, reserve currency status enables the hegemon to expand its strategic ambitions without being constrained by the usual costs of power projection. Wars, alliances, infrastructure aid, and overseas military deployments can be financed at low cost, often with money borrowed from the very countries that are affected by the hegemon's policies. Foreign central banks, in buying the hegemon's bonds, are in essence funding its strategic agenda. This inversion of traditional cost-benefit logic allows the hegemon to act as a global power without bearing proportionate financial risk, a dynamic that perpetuates and amplifies its influence.

Given these benefits, it becomes clear why any hegemon would seek not only to install its own currency as the global reserve but to guard that status jealously. It is not merely a matter of pride or tradition; it is a core pillar of strategic advantage. The risks of losing this status—of allowing another country to rise as the issuer of the dominant currency—are immense. Such a shift would not only erode the hegemon's economic position but threaten its geopolitical dominance. As such, preserving the reserve currency role becomes an objective of national policy, pursued through trade agreements, military alliances, financial diplomacy, and even covert means. Reserve currency is not just a tool of economic convenience—it is a fulcrum of global power. It creates a unique convergence of financial efficiency, political leverage, and strategic autonomy. For the hegemon, the temptation to claim and maintain this status is not a choice—it is an imperative rooted in the logic of power itself. The world may evolve, technologies may change, and new economic powers may rise, but the currency that the world holds in reserve remains, for the time being, the heart of international influence. To relinquish that would be to surrender not just financial advantage, but command over the very structure of the world order.

Chapter 8

Magic

Conventional economic theory warns printing more money inevitably leads to inflation. More money in the system, chasing the same amount of goods and services, should logically push prices upward. However, this simple relationship becomes far more complex in the context of a reserve currency and global trade. When a hegemon prints more of its currency and spends it primarily on foreign imports, the expected outcome is not always inflation. In fact, under certain structural conditions, such actions can generate deflationary pressures, boost domestic asset prices, and even stimulate GDP growth through multiple reinforcing mechanisms. To understand this paradox, one must first grasp the role of imports in this process. When a country with a reserve currency prints more money, it can spend that currency internationally without depleting its foreign reserves or needing to balance trade in the short term. Because its currency is globally accepted, foreign exporters are willing to accept this money in exchange for real goods and services. As a result, the country receives tangible imports—commodities, manufactured goods, technology—while sending abroad newly created money. On the surface, this might appear inflationary. But in practice, the influx of cheap and abundant foreign goods, while domestic money supply hasn't increased, has a powerful downward effect on domestic prices.

The importation of foreign goods in large quantities increases supply in domestic markets, particularly in consumer and industrial sectors. When supply outpaces demand—especially in categories such as electronics, apparel, machinery, and raw materials—prices tend to stabilize or even decline. Moreover, the very act of integrating cheaper imports into a domestic economy forces domestic producers to reduce costs, improve efficiency, or lower their prices to remain competitive. This competition places a lid on domestic inflation and may even contribute to deflationary tendencies in key sectors. Therefore, while the money supply grows, internationally, the effect on price levels is often neutralized or reversed by the overwhelming supply of low-cost goods. In this way, printing money and using it to import foreign goods does not increase prices. The added liquidity, rather than flowing entirely into consumer markets and pushing up prices, is absorbed by an expanding supply chain of imports. The surplus of goods serves as a buffer, preventing excess liquidity from causing overheating in domestic demand. This dynamic explains why reserve currency nations, such as the United States, have often been able to expand their money supply significantly without experiencing proportional increases in consumer price inflation.

At the same time, the monetary expansion and foreign spending stimulate capital inflows. When the hegemon prints money and sends it abroad in exchange for imports, the foreign recipients—whether they are exporting corporations, governments, or central banks—do not simply hold onto this money indefinitely. Much of it returns in the form of investment. Foreign entities convert their dollar earnings into U.S. Treasury securities, equities, real estate, and other financial instruments. In effect, the money used for imports is recycled back into the financial system of the hegemon. This recycling process creates demand for domestic financial assets, driving up their value. This mechanism is critical to understanding why financial markets in reserve currency nations often thrive even amid large trade deficits. The demand for bonds lowers interest rates, supporting credit expansion. The demand for equities pushes up stock prices, generating wealth effects for households and businesses. Rising real estate prices attract even more capital, both foreign and domestic. All of these asset classes become buoyant, not despite the trade imbalance, but because of it. Foreign investment, stimulated by monetary expansion and trade openness, reinforces the upward movement of asset prices in a feedback loop of liquidity and confidence.

Additionally, this cycle has a direct impact on gross domestic product. GDP is not just a measure of what is consumed or exported—it also includes investment, government spending, and the value-added activities that occur domestically. When the hegemon imports foreign goods, it does not merely consume them passively. The process of distributing, marketing, servicing, and integrating those goods into domestic industries creates jobs and economic activity. Ports, logistics firms, retail networks, warehousing, software services, and infrastructure maintenance all benefit from the steady influx of imports. The expansion of these supporting sectors adds to GDP even if the goods themselves are produced abroad. Moreover, foreign investment fueled by recycled reserve currency flows leads to business expansion, research and development, and technological innovation. These activities, though indirectly connected to the original money printing, generate lasting growth. Capital markets become more liquid, firms have easier access to funding, and household wealth grows through rising asset prices. All of this encourages consumption and entrepreneurship, reinforcing the strength of the domestic economy. Thus, the act of printing money and spending it internationally produces a cascade of productive activity that bolsters GDP, often more robustly than direct domestic stimulus.

In fact, it is precisely because the hegemon's currency is in demand that it is able to sustain this system. The ability to import without depleting reserves or devaluing the currency is not available to all countries—only to those whose currency is used as a store of value globally. For most nations, printing money and running persistent trade deficits would eventually lead to inflation, currency depreciation, and capital flight. But for a reserve currency issuer, the global economy becomes a sponge, absorbing excess liquidity through trade and reinvesting it through capital flows. The hegemon becomes a magnet for global surplus savings, able to grow its economy through financial and consumption channels simultaneously. This is not to say there are no risks. The system depends on continued global confidence in the currency and the political stability of the hegemon. It also requires a degree of global economic balance—foreign nations must continue to produce the goods that the hegemon consumes and be willing to reinvest the proceeds. If geopolitical tensions disrupt this equilibrium, or if other countries attempt to challenge the hegemon's currency dominance, the model could face serious strains. Nevertheless, within a stable reserve currency regime, the paradox remains, printing money and spending it abroad may not be inflationary. It may be disinflationary or even deflationary due to the mechanisms of trade, investment, and asset accumulation.

What makes this system particularly powerful is that it is self-reinforcing. The more the hegemon spends abroad, the more foreign nations accumulate its currency. The more they accumulate, the more they invest back in the hegemon's financial markets. The greater the investment, the stronger the financial infrastructure, the higher the asset prices, and the more attractive the hegemon's economy becomes. This cycle, which might appear fragile from the outside, has proven resilient for decades because it is not driven solely by the hegemon's internal policies but by global dependencies on its currency and markets. Monetary expansion directed toward foreign imports does not always produce the inflationary effects predicted by textbook economics. For a reserve currency issuer, such actions can lead to a supply-driven disinflation, a rise in financial asset values due to capital recycling, and a stimulus to GDP through the expansive industries that support trade and investment. The hegemon, by virtue of its monetary position, is able to transform what would otherwise be inflationary into a foundation for economic strength. It is a rare position—one not merely granted by domestic policy but earned through historical trust, institutional strength, and geopolitical dominance. And it is precisely this position that allows the hegemon to rewrite the rules of macroeconomics in its favor.

Chapter 9

Curse

At first glance, holding the status of the world's reserve currency seems like the pinnacle of economic power. The printing press becomes a tool of national strategy, creating a unique privilege that few empires in history have wielded. But this advantage comes with hidden consequences. Over time, the very ease with which the reserve currency is produced and accepted can undermine the health of the productive economy. The empire becomes increasingly reliant on money creation and financial flows, while its traditional industries—manufacturing, agriculture, and even innovation—struggle to compete. What emerges is a quiet affliction, known in economics as "Dutch Disease," but in this case, it is not triggered by a resource boom. It is triggered by financial omnipotence. Dutch Disease refers to a phenomenon first observed in the Netherlands during the 1960s, when the discovery of natural gas and the influx of foreign currency appreciation caused a decline in manufacturing competitiveness.

The term now applies more broadly to situations where a country's currency becomes overvalued due to one dominant sector—typically natural resources—crowding out other sectors through exchange rate pressures and resource misallocation. In the case of a reserve currency issuer, the dominant sector is not oil or gas but finance and sovereign debt. And instead of physical resource extraction, the resource being exploited is the global demand for its money.

In such a system, the central bank and government can expand the money supply almost at will, knowing that foreign institutions, central banks, and investors will absorb the new currency through trade, reserves, and capital flows. The exported money returns in the form of foreign investment, purchases of government bonds, and financial inflows into real estate and equities. This financial ecosystem grows disproportionately large. Banks, asset managers, insurers, and capital markets become the main arteries of the economy. Financial services begin to dominate national GDP, employment, and tax revenues. With money so easily created and financial assets so consistently in demand, policymakers and private actors alike come to view this sector not as a facilitator of the economy but as its engine. Meanwhile, the rest of the economy is quietly strangled. Traditional export industries find it increasingly difficult to compete globally because the reserve currency's value is artificially inflated. Foreign customers struggle to afford the country's goods and services. Domestic firms lose market share not because of inefficiency or poor strategy, but because the cost structure of the economy is skewed by monetary dominance. Wages, property values, and the cost of doing business rise relative to the rest of the world, while profit margins in export sectors shrink. Factories shut down, supply chains move abroad, and the domestic labor market reorients itself toward finance, services, and government.

When printing money is so easy and so effective in generating short-term wealth, the incentive to build long-term productive capacity diminishes. Why invest in factories, agriculture, or R&D when capital can earn higher returns in real estate speculation, equity markets, or sovereign debt? Why develop engineering talent or manufacturing infrastructure when financial instruments can generate wealth faster, safer, and with global demand to back them? Over time, both public and private sectors internalize this logic. Education policy begins to favor business schools and financial degrees. Tax policy rewards capital gains over industrial expansion. Political influence becomes concentrated in financial centers rather than industrial regions. The economy transforms not through conscious design, but through the quiet gravitational pull of easy money. At a certain point, the very notion of economic strength becomes conflated with financial strength. Stock market indexes, home prices, and capital inflows are mistaken for signs of national productivity. But beneath the surface, hollowing out has occurred. The capacity to build and produce real goods has atrophied. Supply chains have been outsourced. Domestic industry is no longer the backbone of national resilience but a faded memory of

a more balanced economy. Strategic sectors become reliant
on imports—sometimes from geopolitical rivals—leaving the
country vulnerable to disruptions it can no longer respond to
with domestic resources. The country can still buy anything,
but it cannot make everything.

What makes this version of Dutch Disease particularly in-
sidious is that it is politically invisible. Unlike inflation or
unemployment, which generate social unrest and political
backlash, the overgrowth of finance often appears beneficial. It supports high asset prices, keeps borrowing costs
low, and sustains consumer confidence. It funds welfare programs and military budgets. And it attracts global capital,
reinforcing the perception of dominance. Politicians have no
incentive to reverse it, and citizens—who see their wealth
grow on paper—have little reason to resist. But slowly, the
empire becomes dependent on its currency status to sustain its standard of living. The economy loses its balance,
and a subtle fragility sets in. Moreover, this dynamic reshapes foreign policy. The need to maintain global demand
for the reserve currency incentivizes the projection of financial systems abroad. It encourages the hegemon to enforce
its monetary architecture through alliances, sanctions, and
military presence. The financial system must be protected
not only at home but globally, lest competitors emerge or
demand falter. Foreign wars and strategic interventions are
often justified not only in terms of security but implicitly as
protectors of the monetary regime. In this way, the domestic Dutch Disease metastasizes into geopolitical overreach,

as the empire's financial needs begin to dictate its global posture.

Eventually, the internal distortions become difficult to reverse. Fiscal austerity risks recession, while stimulus often exacerbates the existing imbalance. The economy becomes a prisoner of its own design. Without its reserve status, it would face a reckoning of devaluation and realignment. With reserve status, it drifts into a slow sclerosis, unable to escape the ease of money and the comfort of finance. This is the paradox of reserve currency privilege; what begins as strength becomes dependency. The very tool that allows an empire to dominate global trade and finance eventually corrupts its domestic foundations. Money becomes too easy, finance too large, and industry too weak. The competitive spirit of capitalism is dulled by the monopolistic comfort of monetary sovereignty. Dutch Disease, in this context, is not just a sectoral misalignment—it is a civilizational drift. While reserve currency status offers immense power and flexibility, it also carries profound structural risks. It invites the temptation of effortless wealth through monetary expansion, which in turn distorts the balance of the economy. Like a nation that discovers oil and forgets how to build machines, a financial empire can forget how to produce. The Dutch Disease that results may not announce itself with a crash or crisis but with a slow erosion of economic vitality.

Chapter 10

Slaved through Strength

When a nation becomes the issuer of the world's reserve currency, it finds itself at the center of the global financial system. Its money is used to settle international trade, its debt is accumulated by foreign central banks, and its financial assets are regarded as safe havens in times of uncertainty. This dominant position brings undeniable privileges—chief among them, the ability to run trade deficits without immediate economic consequence. But hidden within this privilege is a self-reinforcing paradox: the very mechanism that allows a country to flood the world with its currency ends up deepening the trade imbalance it seeks to manage. The reserve currency appreciates in value against others, making imports cheaper and exports less competitive. Attempts to weaken the currency through increased money supply lead not to inflation in traded goods but to inflation in domestic assets and non-tradable goods. As this cycle continues, the country becomes ensnared in a structure from which it cannot easily escape.

Any reserve currency must be supplied in just the right quantities to ensure global markets have enough liquidity to settle trades, manage capital flows, and underwrite cross-border investments. When the world's central banks, multinational corporations, or commodity producers need reserves, they reach for the hegemon's currency. By issuing—or "supplying"—that currency, the issuing nation lubricates international commerce, reduces payment frictions, and underpins confidence in the global financial system. Too little supply chokes trade and drives up borrowing costs; too much risks domestic inflation and erodes the currency's value. The art of reserve-currency stewardship lies in balancing global liquidity needs against home-country stability. The hegemon wields this supply power in three principal ways. First, it can import ever-larger volumes of goods and services, effectively exchanging its printed currency for real-world inputs—from raw materials to cutting-edge technology—that bolster domestic consumption or production. Second, it can recycle that same currency into foreign sovereign debt, purchasing bonds issued by trading partners to both stabilize their markets and earn interest income. Third, and most conservatively, it can acquire hard assets—especially gold—that serve as an immutable store of value and hedge against monetary overexpansion.

Because the reserve currency is in high demand across the globe, its value rises relative to others. This appreciation is not the result of industrial productivity or export surpluses; it is driven by the global desire to hold and transact in that currency. Foreign governments accumulate it as reserves. Corporations use it to settle international contracts. Investors buy the issuing country's debt and equities to store value. As demand rises, the price of the currency increases, and with it, the cost of the country's exports. Goods produced domestically become more expensive to the rest of the world, while foreign goods become cheaper to the reserve currency holders. Over time, this leads to a structural trade imbalance: imports grow, exports shrink, and the country becomes a net consumer of the world's production. Ironically, the very act of importing—which is supposed to increase the global supply of the reserve currency and thereby reduce its value—has the opposite effect. When a country imports more, it sends its currency abroad, expanding foreign holdings. But the nature of these imports, and the low cost at which they are acquired, means they suppress domestic inflation. Cheap goods flood the domestic market, lowering the cost of living and making it appear that monetary expansion has no inflationary cost. Consumers enjoy lower prices, but producers face stiffer competition. Domestic industries are undercut by foreign goods, even as financial institutions flourish by managing the global flow of capital.

Meanwhile, efforts to manage the growing imbalance by increasing the domestic money supply have perverse effects. When central banks expand liquidity, it does not translate into increased competitiveness or stronger exports. Instead, the new money chases financial assets and real estate, whose prices are not constrained by international competition. Stocks, bonds, and housing appreciate rapidly, concentrating wealth in asset-owning classes and amplifying inequality. The consumer price index remains relatively stable because imported goods are inexpensive, but the cost of living rises dramatically through housing, education, and healthcare—sectors that are largely immune to import competition. Thus, monetary easing, intended to lower the value of the currency and boost exports, ends up inflating domestic asset bubbles without correcting, and even worsening, the trade imbalance. This situation is further complicated by the fact that not all goods can be imported. While consumers benefit from cheaper electronics, clothing, and manufactured items, they still face rising prices for goods and services that must be produced locally. Food, housing, utilities, and labor-intensive services become more expensive as financial speculation raises the cost of land, inputs, and wages. For the middle class, the inflation is felt not in televisions or smartphones, but in rent, insurance, and tuition. This dual dynamic—deflation in traded goods and inflation in non-tradables—creates a distorted economy where statistical indicators fail to capture the lived experience of economic pressure.

The resulting imbalance is both external and internal. Externally, the country continues to run trade deficits, exporting money and importing goods. This maintains global demand for the reserve currency, which in turn sustains its high value, keeping imports cheap and exports expensive. Internally, the wealth effect generated by asset inflation leads to over-consumption, underinvestment in productive industries, and growing inequality. The economy becomes less about producing and more about allocating capital. Financialization spreads, not as a deliberate policy, but as a consequence of systemic design. The more the country tries to use monetary policy to regain competitiveness, the more it deepens its dependency on financial flows. This is not an accident or a failure of implementation. It is a structural feature of reserve currency hegemony. The international demand for the currency creates a floor under its value. The country cannot easily devalue its way to competitiveness, because doing so would require reducing its financial attractiveness—an outcome that would unsettle global markets and erode domestic asset values. Similarly, it cannot restrict imports without undermining the very mechanism by which its currency circulates globally. The system requires the country to consume more than it produces, to run deficits as a matter of global necessity. In doing so, it must continue to print money, inflate asset values, and tolerate the erosion of its industrial base.

Over time, this leads to a profound trap. The country cannot stop importing, because its economic model depends on it. It cannot devalue, because its currency is too deeply embedded in the global system. It cannot reverse financialization, because the economy now relies on asset appreciation for growth. Attempts at industrial policy or export revival face insurmountable headwinds from currency strength and wage differentials. Education and infrastructure investment, while important, do not address the deeper problem of structural overvaluation and trade asymmetry. Even protectionism—if politically feasible—risks destabilizing the global trust in the currency itself. This is the invisible burden of reserve currency status. While it may appear as global dominance, it functions more like a subtle dependence. The country must continuously meet the world's demand for its money, which means running deficits and expanding credit. These deficits keep the currency circulating abroad, but they also suppress domestic industry and entrench financial priorities. Every imported good is a double-edged sword: it satisfies domestic demand while further widening the gap between consumption and production. Every increase in the money supply inflates local assets while eroding the affordability of life for the average citizen. The country becomes wealthier on paper but more fragile in substance.

In the end, the trap is psychological as much as it is economic. Policymakers, investors, and even citizens come to view the reserve currency status not just as a privilege, but as an identity. It is seen as proof of strength, even as the foundations of that strength erode. The trade imbalance becomes normalized, the financial bubbles accepted as progress, the decline in manufacturing framed as a shift toward a "service economy." But beneath these narratives lies a deep asymmetry: a nation consuming more than it produces, importing more than it exports, and printing more than it earns. A nation whose global power is sustained by mechanisms that slowly undermine its economic sovereignty. The reserve currency is not simply a tool of international trade or finance. It is a structure that reshapes the entire economy of the issuing nation. It determines what industries rise and fall, what policies are viable, and what futures are possible. It brings immense power—but also immense inertia. And once inside it, a country cannot simply decide to exit. It is not a policy that can be reversed. It is a system that shapes everything around it, until the very idea of change seems impossible.

Chapter 11

The Forge

The transformation of an economy that issues the world's reserve currency is both profound and often misunderstood. At first glance, it appears as a success story: the currency is in demand globally, financial markets are strong, foreign capital flows in, and consumption is abundant. But beneath the surface, this global demand for currency slowly reshapes the structure of the economy itself. The most crucial and often irreversible change is the hollowing out of manufacturing—the very foundation on which the middle class once stood. As factories shut down and skilled labor is devalued, the economy shifts toward financial services and administrative work, creating an inflated service sector that distributes wealth derived not from production but from currency issuance and asset inflation. What follows is the rise of a new kind of economic structure: a hyper-financialized and over-bureaucratized system that masks decline with complexity and consumption. The journey begins with the global de-

mand for the reserve currency. To satisfy this demand, the
issuing country must export its currency in large quantities.
Since most other nations accumulate the reserve currency by
selling goods and services, the reserve country must import
those goods and services in exchange for its currency. This
dynamic creates a persistent trade deficit. On its own, a
trade deficit may not be catastrophic, but over time, as it
becomes structural, it begins to erode the competitive advantage of domestic manufacturing. Foreign producers, operating in environments with lower labor costs and weaker
currencies, are able to sell goods more cheaply than domestic
firms can. Even the most efficient manufacturers struggle to
compete against the flood of inexpensive imports.

As this imbalance grows, domestic manufacturing industries
begin to shrink. Factories that once employed thousands either close or relocate to cheaper regions abroad. Investment
that once flowed into production is redirected into finance,
technology, and services. Towns built around manufacturing slowly decay. Blue-collar workers, once the backbone of
the economy, find themselves with fewer and fewer viable
employment options. The industrial middle class—the engine of upward mobility—begins to disappear, not because
of technological disruption alone, but because the economic
system no longer rewards production. It rewards control
over money. With manufacturing in decline, the economy
turns increasingly to services—not to create wealth through
new value, but to distribute the existing wealth generated by
money printing, asset inflation, and international demand for

the currency. This is not the service economy of craftsmanship, teaching, or innovation. It is the service economy of bureaucracy, finance, compliance, and consulting. A growing share of the workforce becomes involved not in producing goods, but in managing flows of capital, information, and regulation. Bookkeeping replaces building. Administration replaces assembly. The economy becomes layered with oversight and paperwork, not as a matter of necessity, but as a symptom of wealth with no foundation in production.

Financialization takes hold of every sector. Real estate, healthcare, education, and even basic utilities become vehicles for investment rather than necessities of life. Their prices rise far beyond inflation, driven by speculative flows and financial engineering. The goal is no longer to make things more affordable or efficient—it is to extract value from them. Rent-seeking replaces risk-taking. The economy becomes obsessed with managing portfolios, arbitraging interest rates, and leveraging balance sheets. For those with access to capital, it is a golden age. For everyone else, the barriers to entry grow higher by the day. As the financial sector expands, so too does the administrative state. The sheer complexity of managing an economy driven by capital flows rather than production demands a growing class of bureaucrats, analysts, and managers. Government programs, compliance departments, auditing firms, and legal teams proliferate to manage the regulatory, financial, and legal consequences of a hyper-leveraged system. Much of the labor force is drawn into roles that do not create goods or services, but exist to administer the system itself. Paperwork becomes the product. Jobs are created not to fulfill genuine needs, but to maintain the illusion of full employment and social stability.

This bureaucratization has social as well as economic consequences. The dignity of work is redefined. In the industrial age, workers took pride in building things—cars, bridges, machines, homes. They could see the results of their labor and feel their place in a shared national enterprise. In the financial-bureaucratic age, work is abstract, symbolic, often disconnected from tangible outcomes. A meeting replaces a shift. A spreadsheet replaces a lathe. For the professional classes, this abstraction is lucrative; for the displaced working class, it is alienating. Retraining programs and college degrees are offered as solutions, but they often amount to little more than attempts to repackage clerical work as innovation. Meanwhile, the physical infrastructure of the country deteriorates. Roads, railways, power grids, and ports—once central to industrial growth—receive less investment, because they no longer serve the interests of a financialized economy. Real value is created not in factories or shipyards, but in digital platforms and offshore accounts. Supply chains stretch across continents, leaving the country vulnerable to external shocks but reluctant to reindustrialize. Every effort to revive manufacturing faces the same obstacle: the overvalued currency, inflated input costs, and a financial system that favors quick returns over long-term investment.

Attempts to restore balance often fall short, because the structural incentives remain unchanged. Tariffs and subsidies may provide short-term relief, but they do not address the deeper issue: the economy has adapted to a world in which printing money and attracting capital is more profitable than making things. The workforce has been reshaped accordingly. Schools no longer prepare students for technical skills or trades, but for careers in administration, marketing, finance, or law. Apprenticeship is replaced by internships. The culture shifts from one of self-reliance and craftsmanship to one of credentialism and risk aversion. Over time, the reserve currency system produces not a strong, resilient economy, but a fragile, top-heavy one. Wealth is concentrated in financial centers and among asset owners. The majority of the population faces stagnant wages, rising living costs, and declining prospects. Political discontent grows, not just because of inequality, but because of a sense that the system is rigged to reward those who manipulate money rather than those who create value. The social contract frays. Trust in institutions declines. And yet, the country cannot reverse course without risking the collapse of its financial dominance.

Chapter 12

Rusting Hammer

The loss of manufacturing is not just the decline of an economic sector—it is the unraveling of a nation's technological spine, its innovative capacity, and its long-term competitiveness. When an empire grows accustomed to printing money instead of building machines, and to importing products instead of inventing them, it begins to erode the foundation of its technological leadership. This decay is subtle at first, masked by financial growth, asset inflation, and short-term gains. But over time, the consequences accumulate: productivity stagnates, the culture of innovation weakens, and the empire begins to lose its edge—not by conquest, but by complacency. In the early stages, a dominant empire benefits from its position as the issuer of the world's reserve currency. Global demand for its currency ensures capital inflows, which inflate financial markets and support consumption. It imports goods from across the globe, often at prices lower than domestic producers can match. This results in an expanding trade deficit, which seems harmless at first, because the empire can pay for imports with its own currency. The illusion is one of endless prosperity: shelves are full, markets are liquid, and consumer lifestyles remain uninterrupted. But underneath this apparent success, something fundamental is being lost—the industrial ecosystem that once sustained innovation and long-term growth.

Manufacturing is not simply about producing goods; it is about embedding knowledge into physical form. Every machine built, every product assembled, carries with it the refinement of techniques, the solving of problems, and the improvement of processes. The factory floor is where theoretical designs confront material limits. Engineers working alongside technicians and machinists gain insights that no spreadsheet or simulation can replicate. It is in this ecosystem that breakthroughs occur—where materials science meets mechanical precision, where design iterates through hands-on feedback, and where technology advances because the people building it understand its limits intimately. As an empire outsources more and more of its manufacturing, it gradually detaches itself from this learning process. The next generation of engineers and scientists are trained in abstract models rather than applied experience. The skills that once passed from master to apprentice disappear. Technical know-how becomes concentrated in foreign workshops, and with each wave of offshoring, the empire becomes less capable of producing the technologies it once pioneered. It may still dominate in patents or academic research, but these victories are increasingly hollow—disconnected from the material realities of production.

Without manufacturing, innovation becomes theoretical. Research institutions may continue to develop new technologies, but without the infrastructure to produce, test, and scale these innovations, the feedback loop between invention and application breaks down. The process of bringing an idea from the lab to the market requires more than venture capital—it requires industrial capacity, skilled labor, and the cultural memory of how to build. A nation that forgets how to make things loses more than jobs; it loses the very environment in which innovation thrives. Moreover, technological edge is not just a function of individual brilliance—it is a product of collective capacity. The great inventions of the modern world were rarely the work of isolated geniuses. They were the result of coordinated efforts between designers, manufacturers, supply chains, and customers. From the automobile to the jet engine, from the semiconductor to the smartphone, these achievements were made possible by the integration of scientific knowledge with industrial execution. When an empire loses its industrial base, it severs the connective tissue that links discovery to deployment. It may still dream up the next big thing, but someone else will build it—and eventually, someone else will invent it too.

As manufacturing declines, so does competitiveness. The empire begins to lose its ability to respond to economic shocks or geopolitical threats. It becomes dependent on foreign suppliers not just for consumer goods, but for critical technologies—semiconductors, batteries, rare earth components, and medical equipment. This dependency constrains foreign policy, undermines national security, and reduces economic resilience. In a crisis, the inability to produce essential goods becomes a vulnerability that no amount of printed money can fix. At the same time, productivity growth slows. In healthy economies, productivity improves through process optimization, capital investment, and technological upgrades—all of which are tightly connected to manufacturing. When manufacturing disappears, these sources of productivity are weakened. The service sector, which comes to dominate, often lacks the same capacity for productivity gains. While finance, consulting, and digital platforms may generate high profits, they do not replace the deep, compounding returns that come from industrial innovation. Productivity becomes financialized—measured in arbitrage and leverage rather than efficiency and output. The economy grows, but it does not become more capable.

This overreliance on finance also distorts capital allocation. Instead of investing in machinery, R&D, or workforce development, capital flows toward asset speculation, mergers, and stock buybacks. Industrial reinvestment is neglected in favor of short-term returns. The economy becomes risk-averse, chasing yield rather than transformation. Over time, this erodes the entrepreneurial spirit that once drove technological revolutions. Startups that require factories or hardware are starved of capital, while software platforms and financial instruments receive disproportionate funding. The national innovation profile shifts—not toward bold ventures, but toward optimized monetization of existing systems. Eventually, even the most basic components of technological capability begin to decay. Toolmaking, precision engineering, specialized materials, and high-tolerance machining become foreign competencies. The empire becomes a consumer of technology, not a creator. Its military-industrial complex relies on outsourced parts; its infrastructure projects depend on imported equipment; its scientific institutions lack the industrial partners necessary for experimentation and deployment. It becomes increasingly difficult to rebuild the lost capacity, because the skills and infrastructure have vanished. The cost of reshoring manufacturing becomes politically unpalatable, and the cultural memory of how to do it has faded.

Culturally, this transformation leads to a shift in values. A society that once revered builders, engineers, and inventors now celebrates financiers, consultants, and administrators. The pursuit of technical mastery is replaced by credentialism. The pathways to success become narrower, favoring those who manage wealth over those who generate it. Young people are discouraged from entering trades or technical fields, told instead to pursue degrees in management, marketing, or law. The result is a workforce increasingly disconnected from physical reality—well-educated, but poorly equipped to fix, build, or transform the world around them. This erosion of capability is not inevitable, but it is self-reinforcing. Once an economy becomes dependent on imports and financialization, the incentives to reinvest in manufacturing weaken.

Voters demand cheap goods; investors demand quick returns; policymakers fear the short-term costs of reindustrialization. Meanwhile, foreign competitors that retained their manufacturing base continue to advance. They absorb the lessons once learned by the empire, improve upon them, and begin to set the pace of technological change. In time, the empire finds itself not only dependent but behind—struggling to keep up in areas it once dominated.

Chapter 13

Game of Thrones

Capitalism has long been praised as a system that rewards innovation, encourages competition, and increases overall wealth. In theory, it promotes the efficient allocation of resources through the mechanisms of supply and demand. But over time, capitalism has morphed into two very different models. On one side, we have a form of capitalism that serves production—it builds things, creates value, employs people, and contributes to broader prosperity. On the other side, we encounter a form of capitalism that primarily serves itself—it no longer exists to make products or meet needs but rather to maximize wealth for a few by manipulating markets, stifling competition, and distorting democratic processes. The capitalism that serves manufacturing or production is fundamentally aligned with what many consider the original spirit of capitalism. It is rooted in the creation of tangible goods and services. It involves investment in factories, workers, technologies, and supply chains. Companies operating under this model rise or fall based on their ability to deliver better products at better prices. These businesses succeed by increasing efficiency, improving quality, and expanding access. There is a kind of dignity in this model. It relies on effort, skill, and often long-term vision. Profits are reinvested into innovation, expansion, and the training and retention of employees. This form of capitalism has historically played a vital role in lifting millions out of poverty and creating a broad middle class, especially in the post-World War II era.

However, in financialized economies, a different kind of capitalism takes root—a capitalism that no longer exists to produce or innovate, but rather to manipulate the system in its own favor. This version of capitalism is extractive. It is not interested in manufacturing products or generating value through innovation. Its main tools are financial engineering, regulatory capture, monopolistic practices, and political influence. The objective is no longer to win by being better, but to ensure no one else has the opportunity to compete. This self-serving capitalism uses money and power not as tools of innovation but as weapons of control. Large corporations and financial institutions, often flush with capital, spend vast resources on lobbying efforts to shape laws and regulations in their favor. They seek tax loopholes, suppress labor costs, resist antitrust enforcement, and pressure policymakers to ensure their continued dominance. In doing so, they create environments where competition is not just discouraged—it is actively crushed.

Startups and small businesses, which once formed the bedrock of economic dynamism, now struggle to survive in markets dominated by a handful of giants. These smaller players often cannot compete, not because they lack talent or vision, but because the rules of the game have been rewritten to favor incumbents. Barriers to entry are not just technological or capital-based—they are legal, regulatory, and political. At the same time, this form of capitalism contributes significantly to rising wealth inequality. Since it does not depend on productive labor or broad economic participation, it concentrates wealth in the hands of a few. Profits are not shared among workers or reinvested in communities—they are often funneled into stock buybacks, executive bonuses, and speculative financial assets. The average worker sees stagnant wages even as corporate profits soar and executive compensation reaches astronomical levels. Meanwhile, capital gains—income derived from investments rather than labor—are taxed at lower rates, reinforcing the divide between those who live off their labor and those who live off their capital.

Wealth disparity, once a side effect, has become a feature of this extractive capitalism. It creates a self-reinforcing cycle: wealth buys political influence, which leads to policies that protect and grow that wealth, which in turn increases influence. The result is a system where the playing field is tilted, and where upward mobility becomes the exception rather than the rule. Moreover, this type of capitalism distorts the very idea of value. In a manufacturing-based model, value is relatively clear—you make a product, provide a service, meet a need. But in extractive capitalism, value is often created through perception, manipulation, and financial abstraction. It is not unusual for companies that produce little or nothing of tangible worth to achieve enormous valuations based on speculative metrics. Financial markets reward short-term gains and punish long-term thinking. Entire business models are built around arbitrage, speculation, and rent-seeking rather than production.

The dangers of this system go beyond economics. When capitalism begins to serve itself rather than society, it undermines democracy. Political power becomes concentrated among the wealthy. Regulatory agencies are captured by the industries they are supposed to oversee. The voices of ordinary citizens are drowned out by the moneyed interests. This weakens the foundations of democratic governance and fuels widespread disillusionment. People begin to feel, often rightly, that the system is rigged against them. This erodes social trust and creates fertile ground for political instability and populist backlash. Historically, societies have faced similar challenges. The Gilded Age of the late 19th century in the United States, for instance, saw the rise of powerful monopolies and vast wealth disparities. It took a combination of progressive political movements, labor organizing, and antitrust enforcement to rebalance the system. The New Deal reforms of the 1930s similarly attempted to curb the excesses of unfettered capitalism after the Great Depression. In both cases, political will and social pressure were essential in shifting capitalism back toward production and away from extraction.

Chapter 14

Inherited Chains

When a country issues the global reserve currency, it does not simply engage in the exchange of goods for paper. What it sends out into the world is far more consequential: it sells its future. Every unit of currency that leaves the country and enters the coffers of foreign governments, investment funds, and global corporations represents a claim on its real assets—its debt, its land, its companies, and ultimately, its people's labor and productivity. The privilege of being able to print money that the rest of the world accepts is not a gift without cost; it is a bargain that slowly mortgages a nation's future in exchange for present comfort. In the early days of reserve currency dominance, this arrangement can feel like magic. Goods from across the world flow into the reserve country. High-quality electronics, raw materials, consumer products, and even labor-intensive services are exchanged for currency that the reserve country alone can produce at will. Foreigners, in turn, accept this currency because they

believe in its stability, its convertibility, and most of all, its
utility in global markets. Central banks accumulate it to
stabilize their own currencies. Exporters accept it in return
for goods. Investors park their wealth in the reserve country's financial markets. At first glance, it appears to be a
perfect transaction—the world receives a reliable medium of
exchange, and the reserve country receives global goods and
foreign investment. But this relationship is not a closed cycle. The currency that leaves the country does not vanish.
It circulates globally and returns home in the form of foreign
claims.

Foreign central banks use their reserves to buy government
bonds. Global corporations buy up commercial property,
companies, and strategic assets. Wealthy individuals invest
in real estate, universities, and stock markets. Sovereign
wealth funds take ownership stakes in domestic enterprises.
All of this is made possible by the initial issuance of currency and debt. The reserve country, in essence, provides
the world with money, and the world returns with ownership. This process slowly but inexorably shifts control.
The reserve country becomes a host to foreign capital. It
opens itself up to financial infiltration not through conquest,
but through invitation. To maintain its currency's dominance, it must run persistent trade deficits—sending more
currency abroad than it receives. These deficits are funded
through borrowing. Over time, the national debt grows, and
with it, the interest obligations that must be paid to foreign
holders. A growing share of the country's fiscal output is

redirected not toward domestic needs, but toward maintaining the illusion of financial strength and the global demand for its currency. As debt accumulates, the country finds itself constrained. Policymakers must keep interest rates low to manage debt servicing costs. Any aggressive monetary tightening risks triggering a financial crisis, both domestically and abroad. The reserve country becomes a prisoner of its own status—unable to conduct policy primarily for its own people, because the stability of the global system depends on its compliance. The very institutions that once underpinned sovereignty—its central bank, its treasury, its regulators—now operate with an eye toward global markets, foreign investors, and external stakeholders.

Real estate prices, inflated by foreign capital, push citizens out of their own cities. The influx of external money distorts local markets, turning homes into speculative assets and pricing out entire generations. Industries that once served national interests are restructured to satisfy foreign shareholders. Strategic decisions about labor, production, and innovation are made not for national competitiveness, but for quarterly returns. Sovereignty is eroded not by treaties or wars, but by the logic of capital. This erosion is most visible in the nation's inability to control its own destiny. When a crisis arises, foreign capital becomes a liability. Investors can withdraw with alarming speed, triggering collapses in asset prices, exchange rates, and consumer confidence. To prevent this, the reserve country must continuously reassure the world—through monetary support, fiscal credibility, and international diplomacy—that it remains a safe harbor. It is no longer simply governing itself; it is performing stability for a global audience.

And yet, the warning signs are always present. Each financial crisis reveals how exposed the system has become. Each recession shows the fragility of an economy dependent on inflows of capital and cheap imports. Each geopolitical tension raises the question, what happens if the world no longer wants the reserve currency? What if the promises made through the sale of bonds and issuance of money cannot be kept? What if foreign holders lose confidence—not just in the currency, but in the country behind it? At that moment, the reserve currency is no longer a source of strength but a source of vulnerability. The tools that once bought global influence now bring instability. The debts that once seemed manageable now become unpayable. The wealth that seemed infinite is revealed to be borrowed. And the future—once mortgaged for the sake of present comfort—demands repayment.

To sell one's currency to the world is to invite it into one's home. To finance consumption through debt is to place the burden on tomorrow's workers. To run deficits in exchange for imported goods is to trade industrial resilience for global status. These are choices made not all at once, but through decades of policy, habit, and economic theory. Yet each choice accumulates. And together, they shape the destiny of the nation. The reserve currency is not just money. It is a claim on real things—on land, labor, and institutions. It allows a country to delay difficult decisions, but not to escape them. It allows prosperity to be maintained artificially, but not indefinitely. Eventually, the future comes due. And when it does, a nation must reckon with what it has sold, what it has lost, and what it must do to reclaim its sovereignty.

Chapter 15

Opium of Peasants

A reserve currency grants a nation remarkable powers—among them, the ability to finance its needs not through production and export, but through the effortless issuance of its own money. When that currency is globally accepted, the usual constraints that bind other countries—budgetary discipline, export competitiveness, labor efficiency—can be relaxed, even ignored. Goods and services can be imported at will. Deficits can be sustained indefinitely. Foreigners line up to buy bonds, invest in assets, and park their savings in the reserve country's markets. For a time, it feels like economic gravity no longer applies. But what begins as a privilege eventually becomes a trap, not just economically but psychologically. Over time, the ease of printing money breeds a culture of laziness, entitlement, and collective detachment from the hard truths of production, effort, and value.

In any healthy economy, wealth is the product of work. It

must be earned through innovation, toil, and enterprise. A society must cultivate skills, nurture industry, and compete on the global stage. Its people must understand that prosperity is fragile and requires constant renewal. But when a nation can print what others must earn, those instincts atrophy. The urgency to innovate gives way to complacency. The drive to work hard fades beneath the comfort of easy living. A growing segment of society comes to believe that wealth is a birthright, not a result of discipline and sacrifice. They begin to view a high standard of living as a fact of life, not a consequence of effort or competition. The conveniences of reserve currency status—cheap imports, strong financial markets, a globally accepted currency—are taken for granted, as though they were gifts of geography or history, not privileges secured through generations of responsibility.

As this attitude permeates, it shapes both public opinion and policy. The political class learns that it is easier to promise than to produce. Social programs are expanded, not based on what the economy can sustainably support, but on what can be funded through borrowing. Political discourse becomes a competition of giveaways—free education, healthcare, housing, subsidies, tax cuts—all financed by debt, with little concern for the long-term consequences. The central bank becomes the engine of social peace, printing money to support markets, bail out corporations, and indirectly fund public spending. The message, slowly absorbed by the public, is clear: there is always more money. There is no price to be paid. In such an environment, economic hardship becomes alien. Recession is not a natural phase of the cycle, but a political scandal. The idea of austerity, of tightening belts and enduring short-term pain for long-term health, becomes politically untenable. Citizens demand constant growth, ever-rising asset prices, and the preservation of consumption at all costs. Any disruption—whether from global instability, natural disaster, or economic mismanagement—is met with demands for immediate compensation. Stimulus checks, bailouts, moratoriums, and subsidies are no longer emergency tools—they become expected responses, almost automatic. The line between need and entitlement fades.

A society accustomed to having the world's products at its fingertips begins to devalue the effort that went into them. People lose touch with the supply chains, labor, and innovation that bring goods to their shelves. A smartphone, a car, a shipment of food, are no longer seen as marvels of coordination, industry, and global trade. They are assumed, and any disruption to their flow is viewed as an injustice. The labor that once underpinned the nation's wealth—manufacturing, agriculture, infrastructure—becomes invisible. These industries shrink, often outsourced to cheaper regions, while domestic labor shifts toward services, entertainment, and administration. The service economy, buoyed by printed money and inflated financial assets, creates an illusion of vitality. Job growth appears in sectors like consulting, education, finance, government, and healthcare administration. But much of this is enabled by the underlying financial expansion.

As long as the currency is accepted abroad, and borrowing remains cheap, these sectors grow. Yet they often add limited productive value. They circulate wealth rather than create it. In the absence of real constraints, many roles become bloated, inefficient, and detached from any measurable outcome. The bureaucracy of the economy expands, staffed by people whose livelihoods depend not on market feedback, but on institutional inertia and government budgets.

At the personal level, the effect is more subtle but no less profound. Young people grow up in a society where working with one's hands is undervalued, where domestic production is rare, and where digital wealth creation seems far more attractive than building physical things. The idea of struggle—starting from the bottom, building a business, learning a trade—is replaced by dreams of financial windfalls, influencer careers, and speculative investing. Cultural narratives celebrate passive income, portfolio gains, and lifestyle optimization. Hard work is no longer honored unless it produces fame or fortune. An entire generation grows up believing that the comforts of reserve currency status are the natural baseline of life. Over time, this culture becomes self-reinforcing. Education focuses on management rather than mastery, on analysis rather than action. Universities prepare students not to build but to administer. Business models are designed not around long-term value but short-term financial engineering. Consumers lose their ability to distinguish between needs and wants, between earned wealth and borrowed prosperity. The nation begins to mirror its financial system: high in volume but low in substance, driven by appearances more than fundamentals.

A society raised on ease is unprepared for hardship. A population that views stability as permanent cannot adapt when it ends. When the moment inevitably arrives—when inflation surges, or borrowing becomes constrained, or the reserve status is questioned—the public is caught off guard. They do not have the tools, the habits, or the mindset to respond. The entitlement that once provided comfort now becomes a source of fragility. Resilience must be rebuilt from scratch, often under the pressure of crisis. A reserve currency is a powerful tool. But when its power is used to avoid pain, to delay change, and to mask weakness, it becomes a drug. It numbs a society to its own decline. It allows the decay of competitiveness, the erosion of industry, the loss of financial discipline—all while keeping the illusion of strength. The true cost is not borne by the present generation but by the next, who inherit the hollowed-out shell of a once-great economy, and who must relearn, through difficulty and sacrifice, what their predecessors forgot. The comforts of a reserve currency are not sustainable unless they are earned and renewed. If they are treated as entitlements, they become chains. And a nation that confuses privilege with permanence, that mistakes convenience for invincibility, will one day awaken to a world where its money is no longer enough—where the real wealth it once had is gone, and all that remains is the memory of a time when printing paper seemed like power.

Chapter 16

Iron Fist

When a nation controls the world's reserve currency, it possesses a level of financial and geopolitical power that is unmatched in human history. This status grants the central government influence not only over its own economy but over the economies of virtually every other nation. Through control of global capital flows, monetary policy, and trade networks, the reserve currency issuer becomes a gravitational center of global finance. However, with this power comes the temptation to overreach, to manipulate the system for narrow national gains, and to impose terms on others who lack the same leverage. Over time, these actions do not go unnoticed. They create resentment among other countries, many of which feel trapped in an arrangement where their labor, resources, and savings are subordinated to a system they do not control. As the reserve currency nation exercises its dominance through sanctions, asset freezes, and political coercion, trust in the impartiality and reliability of its finan-

cial system begins to deteriorate. What begins as privilege
can eventually breed discontent, and the very power that
sustains a reserve currency may ultimately sow the seeds of
its rejection.

Domestically, the central government of a reserve currency
nation enjoys unique privileges that allow it to operate far
beyond the constraints faced by most other governments.
It can run persistent fiscal and trade deficits without facing immediate consequences, because global demand for its
currency and debt absorbs the cost. This enables the government to finance wars, social programs, and corporate res-
cues without significantly raising taxes or cutting spending.
The treasury, supported by the central bank, can inject liquidity, redirect capital, and influence markets with minimal
resistance. As foreign capital flows in to purchase government bonds and goods, trade deficits are normalized and
even welcomed, since cheap imports keep consumption high
while masking structural weaknesses. Over time, this arrangement shifts economic control into the hands of a small
group of government officials who increasingly bypass the
democratic feedback mechanisms typically enforced through
taxation and public debate.

This concentration of power undermines the foundational
principles of representative government. When the state
no longer needs to justify its spending through taxation,
it also stops needing to justify its priorities to its citizens.
Democratic institutions, once vital in balancing public needs
with limited resources, lose influence as fiscal decisions are

made without electoral consequences. This detachment fosters complacency, inefficiency, and often corruption, while sidelining the voices of those who ultimately bear the social and economic impacts. A government that can print and borrow without restraint begins to act more like an empire than a republic—less accountable, more insulated, and increasingly detached from the people it claims to serve. This consolidation of domestic power leads to distortions in policy priorities. Political leaders become more responsive to the needs of financial markets than to the long-term health of the nation. And because the money supply can always be expanded without immediate domestic inflation, there is little constraint on spending.

Internationally, the reserve currency country commands enormous power over the global economy. Because so many international transactions—from oil purchases to sovereign debt repayments—are denominated in its currency, it can influence the terms of trade, set the rules of global finance, and dictate the behavior of other nations. Countries must acquire and hold its currency to function in global markets. Central banks around the world stockpile its bonds as reserves. Multinational corporations settle their accounts using its banking infrastructure. Global supply chains are denominated in its monetary terms. In effect, the reserve currency nation becomes the clearinghouse of the world—a role that offers tremendous leverage. But this leverage is not without consequences. Other countries often find themselves in a subordinate position. The labor and resources of one part of the world are effectively transformed into claims on the consumption of another. In this arrangement, it is easy for resentment to grow. Workers in developing nations may come to view themselves as part of an exploitative system in which their effort is undervalued. Governments may feel pressured to align with the geopolitical interests of the reserve currency nation or risk financial isolation.

This imbalance becomes especially stark in times of crisis or conflict. The reserve currency country can—and often does—weaponize its financial infrastructure. It can unilaterally impose sanctions that freeze the assets of foreign leaders, companies, or entire nations. It can exclude banks from the global payments network. It can seize reserves held abroad. And because of the currency's centrality in global trade, these measures are often devastating. They paralyze economies, drive up the cost of basic goods, and cause mass unemployment. While such tools may be justified on moral or security grounds, their arbitrary application creates a chilling effect. Nations begin to question the neutrality of the financial system. They wonder whether their assets are truly safe, whether their contracts will be honored, or whether their economies can function independently. Each new sanction, seizure, or asset freeze chips away at the perception that the reserve currency system is fair, stable, and apolitical.

The long-term consequence of this power imbalance is a breakdown of trust. Trust is the foundation of any currency's value—especially a reserve currency. It is not backed by gold, oil, or factories. It is backed by the belief that it will remain liquid, stable, and widely accepted. But when other nations begin to see the reserve currency not as a neutral instrument but as a tool of coercion, that belief erodes. Alternatives begin to emerge. Countries explore bilateral trade agreements in local currencies. Regional blocs develop payment systems that bypass the traditional financial hubs. Central banks diversify their reserves. Gold, once dismissed as obsolete, returns to favor. Slowly but surely, a global effort takes shape to reduce dependency on a single dominant currency. Ironically, the very success of the reserve currency system creates the conditions for its decline. The centralization of power leads to overuse. The benefits it confers become incentives for short-term exploitation rather than long-term stewardship. And the resentment it generates motivates others to seek alternatives. No empire lasts forever, and no currency retains dominance without responsibility.

Chapter 17

Lords and knights

In any economic system, there is always some degree of inequality. But in a nation that controls the world's reserve currency, inequality becomes structural, persistent, and inevitable. This is not merely the result of natural market forces or talent disparities. Rather, it is deeply rooted in the very design of the system—a design where the creation of money, the flow of credit, and the distribution of capital are increasingly controlled by a small group of institutions and individuals who sit close to the "printer." The closer one is to this center of monetary power, the more access they have to freshly created capital before it diffuses into the broader economy. Over time, this access becomes the single most important determinant of wealth. As the financial system becomes more central to national life and the productive base shrinks, a dangerous economic dynamic takes shape: wealth clusters around insiders, while the rest of the population is left behind. In traditional economic theory, wealth is earned by creating value—building goods, providing services, solving problems. But in a reserve currency empire, the rules change. Because the nation can create its own money and spend it globally with minimal consequences, the incentive to produce real goods fades. Instead, value is increasingly extracted through financial mechanisms—managing capital, speculating on assets, issuing debt, or allocating public funds. Those who are positioned to influence these flows—whether as government officials, media figures, military contractors, or financial professionals—find themselves at the nexus of wealth creation. They are not creating value in the old industrial sense. They are capturing it.

The result is a lopsided society where money no longer follows merit or labor, but access and connections. The most lucrative jobs are no longer those that require mastery over materials, machines, or even ideas. They are those that involve proximity to capital. The banker who arranges government bond sales, the bureaucrat who manages budget allocations, the consultant who advises on policy rollouts—all of these figures benefit from a system that rewards coordination with the money printer rather than independent economic contribution. Their wealth is not the result of market-tested success. It is the byproduct of their institutional role within a system of easy money. This dynamic reinforces itself. As money creation becomes more central to the economy, the financial industry grows disproportionately. Investment banks, hedge funds, private equity firms, and real estate developers—many of which depend heavily on low-interest debt and public liquidity—dominate the upper layers of income and asset ownership. These firms attract talent not necessarily because they offer the most innovative work, but because they sit closest to the capital spigot. Their profits are leveraged by access to cheap credit, financial opacity, and regulatory capture. The financialization of the economy means that talent migrates away from manufacturing, science, or engineering and into money management. The pursuit of wealth is no longer a race to create but a scramble to allocate.

Meanwhile, the middle class—the historical backbone of national prosperity—faces a different reality. Their industries have been hollowed out by globalization, automation, and financial speculation. Factories have shut down. Domestic supply chains have atrophied. Industrial towns have withered. These workers are not connected to capital markets. They do not have access to insider information, revolving doors, or lobbying networks. They do not benefit from asset inflation because they own few assets. Their wages are stagnant, and their savings are eroded by cycles of boom and bust driven by monetary policy far beyond their control. Even entrepreneurship—once a path to upward mobility—is distorted by this dynamic. In a healthy economy, entrepreneurs compete on the basis of innovation, efficiency, and product quality. But in a financialized reserve currency empire, startups often compete for access to funding rather than customers. Venture capital, subsidies, and government contracts shape which businesses succeed, not necessarily market feedback. As a result, entrepreneurship becomes another channel of gatekeeping, where success depends on networks and connections rather than creativity or grit. Those outside the circles of capital remain locked out.

Over time, this economic structure alters the culture of the country. Positions in government, media, and finance are no longer seen as public services or neutral professions. They become perceived—and often rightly so—as pathways to private enrichment. The revolving door between regulatory agencies and Wall Street, between defense departments and military contractors, between public office and lobbying firms, becomes a defining feature of national life. The incentives are clear: serve the system, and the system will take care of you. The job is not to question the arrangement but to align with it. The result is a society in which loyalty to the financial system becomes more profitable than loyalty to the productive economy. Resentment grows. The middle class begins to see the upper class not as more capable or deserving, but as complicit in a rigged system. Young people entering the workforce feel the gap between aspiration and reality widening. They are told that hard work and education will lead to success, but they see the largest fortunes made through financial arbitrage, regulatory capture, or political access. Disillusionment sets in. The narrative of upward mobility weakens. Trust in institutions declines. Cynicism spreads. In such an environment, even well-meaning reforms struggle to take root, as the public perceives them as cosmetic gestures rather than structural changes.

A society divided by money is also divided by worldview. Those at the top begin to live in a different reality—physically, socially, and intellectually. Their neighborhoods are safer, their schools are better, their access to healthcare and opportunity is wider. They interact with the world through the lens of capital, abstracted from the day-to-day struggles of ordinary life. Meanwhile, the rest of the population experiences growing insecurity, housing instability, healthcare stress, and a constant sense of falling behind. The idea of national unity becomes harder to maintain. The lived experience of one part of the country no longer resembles that of another. Eventually, such inequality becomes not only unjust but unsustainable. Economic systems require legitimacy. When the public no longer believes that the system rewards effort and honesty, when they see wealth concentrated among insiders while the majority struggles, the social fabric begins to unravel. Calls for reform become louder. Political polarization increases. Radical ideologies gain traction. The trust that underpins markets and institutions erodes. And in the background, the privileges of reserve currency status—which once allowed the nation to live beyond its means—begin to weaken as other countries reevaluate their participation in an unjust system.

Chapter 18

Borrowed Swords

Military power is not merely the result of troop numbers, weapon stockpiles, or the amount of money a nation allocates to defense. At its core, it is the projection of industrial and technological might. Every plane that flies, every ship that sails, and every missile that launches is the product of countless hours of engineering, machining, precision manufacturing, testing, and technological refinement. An empire's ability to sustain its military, expand its reach, and defend its interests across the world depends not on how much money it prints, but on the real economy that supports the war machine—factories, supply chains, skilled labor, and a culture of innovation. When that real economy is neglected or hollowed out, the military will eventually suffer, no matter how large the defense budget appears on paper.

Historically, the most powerful militaries have always emerged from nations with strong manufacturing bases. During the

Second World War, for example, it was not only the bravery of Allied soldiers that defeated fascism, but also the factories of Detroit, Pittsburgh, and Chicago. American assembly lines churned out tanks, planes, trucks, and ammunition at a scale the world had never seen. Steel production, shipbuilding, and aircraft manufacturing became the beating heart of the war effort. It was industrial supremacy that allowed military supremacy. The logistics of war, the maintenance of supply chains, and the speed of replenishment all depended on having a fully functioning, highly skilled, and resilient industrial foundation. Technology, too, is inseparable from military power. The radar, the jet engine, the atomic bomb—all revolutionary military tools of the twentieth century—originated in civilian research centers, universities, and industrial laboratories. The integration between civilian technological research and military application made it possible to constantly modernize and adapt in response to new threats. A nation that invests in science and engineering, and retains a robust domestic capability to produce what it invents, holds a decisive edge on the battlefield.

But as an empire grows wealthy from the privileges of issuing the world's reserve currency, it begins to neglect the very foundation of its power. It no longer needs to produce in order to consume. It no longer needs to export to balance its books. It can simply print money and import what it needs from others. In the short term, this appears efficient. Goods are cheaper, inflation is suppressed, and capital is freed up for consumption. But over time, the consequences become clear. Factories close. Skilled workers are laid off. Engineering expertise erodes. Supply chains are outsourced to foreign countries. Manufacturing towns decay, and the next generation loses the incentive to enter technical trades. With each passing year, the empire becomes less self-reliant, less capable of producing for itself, and more dependent on a global supply chain it no longer controls. Without domestic manufacturing, the military becomes reliant on foreign suppliers for parts, components, and even raw materials. Ships, tanks, and aircraft may still be designed at home, but their components are scattered across the globe. A jet might require semiconductors from Taiwan, rare earth elements from China, specialized metals from Africa, or electronic subsystems from European contractors. In a stable world, this might seem manageable. But in a world of rising geopolitical tension, this level of dependence is a serious vulnerability. What happens when war breaks out, and those supply lines are cut? What happens when a foreign country decides to withhold a critical resource? What happens when your rivals control the very components needed to build your weapons?

Moreover, as the economy shifts from production to finance, the culture that once supported military innovation begins to change. The brightest minds no longer go into engineering or physics—they go into finance, consulting, or tech platforms. They are drawn not to solve the nation's hardest problems, but to optimize algorithms for ad revenue or manage portfolios. Research funding tilts away from foundational science and toward quick, marketable innovations. Defense contrac-

tors, once builders of complex systems, increasingly become
project managers who rely on subcontractors and foreign
vendors. Military procurement becomes slower, costlier, and
more bureaucratic, with fewer breakthroughs and more de-
lays. The hardware becomes more expensive and less reliable, while software vulnerabilities mount. The cutting edge
dulls. Even when defense budgets are increased, the results
are disappointing. More money is thrown at outdated systems, inefficient contractors, and projects that run over budget and underdeliver. The illusion of strength persists—after
all, the numbers look large—but the underlying capability is
eroding. An aircraft carrier may cost billions, but if its planes
rely on foreign chips or if its construction is delayed by steel
shortages or labor disputes, its effectiveness is compromised.
A missile may look fearsome, but if it can't be produced at
scale or maintained without imported parts, it is a liability,
not an asset.

The military's operational flexibility suffers as well. The
ability to surge production during a crisis, replenish muni-
tions quickly, or adapt equipment for new theaters of war all
depend on having domestic manufacturing capacity. Without it, the military becomes rigid. It can fight a short war,
but not a long one. It can respond to one crisis, but not
multiple. It can deploy forces, but cannot sustain them. Its
strength becomes performative rather than practical. Furthermore, the reliance on imported goods—even for the military—erodes national sovereignty. If your army cannot march
without foreign components, then your foreign policy is con-

strained. You may hesitate to take a stand against a rival that supplies your rare earth metals. You may find yourself making concessions in trade or diplomacy simply to keep the flow of materials going. Economic interdependence may be good for peace in theory, but in practice, it makes an empire vulnerable to blackmail, manipulation, and strategic ambiguity. Military independence requires economic independence—and that is impossible without manufacturing independence.

When an empire no longer produces what it needs to defend itself, it loses confidence. Its leaders grow accustomed to outsourcing not only goods but also responsibility. They become dependent on defense contractors, intelligence agencies, and technocratic bureaucracies to manage military affairs. The civilian-military divide widens. The public becomes detached from the realities of war and defense, and the military becomes an insular institution, sustained by money but isolated from the broader society. This gap creates mistrust, misunderstanding, and eventually, mismanagement. Strategy suffers. Coordination falters. The empire can no longer act with coherence or decisiveness. Over time, rival powers that retain their manufacturing and technological capacities begin to catch up. They may not have the reserve currency, but they have factories, engineers, and discipline. They invest in dual-use industries, train skilled labor, and develop their own military-industrial base. Slowly but surely, they narrow the gap. The reserve currency empire, meanwhile, continues to rely on financial engineering and legacy systems. It becomes complacent, believing that its past dominance guarantees future supremacy. It underestimates its competitors and overestimates its own resilience. By the time it realizes the balance has shifted, it may already be too late.

Chapter 19

Decadence

At the height of an empire's economic strength there is a dangerous illusion that money is infinite. After all, if foreign countries demand your currency to facilitate international trade, and global institutions hold your debt as the benchmark of stability, then printing money or issuing bonds seems harmless. Governments begin to spend without constraint. Welfare programs are expanded, military budgets balloon, bureaucracies grow, and political promises multiply. For a while, it works. There are no immediate consequences. The economy appears to thrive, stock markets rise, unemployment falls, and interest rates remain low. But beneath the surface, a structural imbalance is forming—an expanding gap between national income and national debt. This is the beginning of the spending spree era, where money is cheap, credit is abundant, and discipline is forgotten. Governments no longer treat debt as a temporary tool for emergencies but as a perpetual instrument for sustaining the illusion of

prosperity. Every shortfall in revenue is covered by borrowing. Every political problem is met with a spending solution.
Deficits are normalized, and any voice of caution is dismissed
as outdated or pessimistic. The central bank, either explic-
itly or implicitly, supports this behavior through monetary
easing, asset purchases, and the constant promise that interest rates will stay low forever.

While the currency issuer can borrow in its own currency
and theoretically never default, it cannot escape the underlying laws of finance and confidence. When budget and trade
deficit grow wider year after year, it means that future productivity is being sacrificed for present consumption. The
nation's capacity to generate real output—goods, services,
innovation—is being outpaced by its financial obligations.
At first, this seems manageable, because interest payments
are low. But as the total debt stock rises, even a small increase in interest rates has outsized effects on the cost of servicing the debt. Eventually, the burden becomes too heavy
to ignore. As investors begin to question the sustainability
of government finances, interest rates start rising. It is not
merely a function of central bank policy anymore—it is the
market itself demanding higher returns for higher risk. The
cost of borrowing climbs. Debt refinancing becomes more
expensive. A larger and larger portion of government revenue goes toward interest payments, leaving less for essential
services or productive investment. The government is caught
in a trap: raising taxes or cutting spending would shrink the
economy and cause social unrest; continuing to borrow would

further inflate the debt burden and undermine confidence.

At this stage, the decline becomes visible even to those who once dismissed the warnings. The symptoms are unmistakable: persistent inflation in core goods, stagnation in wages, widening wealth gaps, deteriorating public services, and rising distrust in institutions. Every faction of society begins to act defensively. The wealthy move their capital offshore or into hard assets. The middle class demands subsidies and debt relief. Corporations lobby for protection or bailouts. Political groups fight over the spoils, each trying to secure a larger share before the pie shrinks further. This collective scramble accelerates the breakdown. Investment dries up. Innovation slows. The currency begins to wobble. Populism finds fertile ground in such an environment. When the public feels betrayed by elites, and when promises of endless prosperity are exposed as hollow, demagogues rise. They blame foreigners, immigrants, financial elites, or political opponents for the crisis. They offer simple answers to complex problems. Protectionism becomes a popular tool. Tariffs are introduced in the name of saving domestic jobs. Imports are demonized, and foreign competition is vilified. The intention is to rebuild local industry and restore self-sufficiency—but the execution often backfires.

Protectionist policies may provide temporary relief to select industries, but they generally reduce competitiveness in the long run. Without foreign competition, local producers lose the pressure to innovate or improve. Costs rise, quality stagnates, and consumers suffer. Tariffs trigger retaliation, harming exporters and straining international relationships. Trade slows, investment declines, and growth falters. Instead of revitalizing the economy, protectionism often isolates it. What was once a vibrant, globally integrated powerhouse begins to resemble a defensive, shrinking fortress. Meanwhile, the debt continues to mount. The government, unwilling or unable to enact real reforms, keeps borrowing. It issues bonds to pay off old bonds. The central bank, now politically compromised or desperate to avoid a financial crisis, resumes aggressive monetary expansion. But this time, the effect is different. The new money no longer stimulates growth—it fuels asset bubbles, further distorts wealth distribution, and pushes inflation in areas where supply cannot respond, such as housing, healthcare, and education. The working class is squeezed. The young see no future. The old worry about their savings. Social cohesion begins to fray.

Confidence in the currency starts to erode internationally. Foreign holders of the reserve currency, once happy to accumulate it as a store of value or medium of exchange, begin to diversify. Central banks reduce their holdings. Sovereign wealth funds reallocate. Private investors look elsewhere for safety. Demand for the reserve currency weakens, not catastrophically, but steadily. As the currency's global dominance fades, the empire's ability to finance its deficits externally is diminished. More debt must now be absorbed domestically, raising interest costs and crowding out private investment. The feedback loop tightens. Strategic planning becomes politicized, and geopolitical influence wanes. Former allies question commitments. Rivals grow more assertive. Domestically, the population becomes more polarized. Political debate degenerates into tribal conflict. Compromise becomes impossible. The institutions that once upheld stability—courts, legislatures, media—become battlegrounds. Trust erodes. Cynicism rises. Leaders govern through spectacle rather than substance, using short-term fixes to distract from long-term decay. Democracy, if it exists, becomes hollow. The very machinery of governance is corroded by debt and divided by resentment. This stage of decline is not dramatic or sudden. It unfolds gradually, like a slow-motion collapse. From the outside, the empire may still appear wealthy and powerful. Its cities may be lit up, its entertainment industry vibrant, its universities prestigious. But underneath, the foundation is crumbling.

The economic engine is sputtering, the social fabric is tearing, and the political order is unraveling. The reserve currency, once a symbol of trust and strength, becomes a relic of a system that no longer works. And yet, in this moment of truth, there is often no consensus about what went wrong. Some blame foreign competitors, others blame capitalism, or immigration, or globalization. Few acknowledge the deeper truth: that the empire overreached, mistook financial privilege for real strength, and abandoned the hard work of building, producing, and innovating. It chose comfort over discipline, consumption over investment, and spectacle over substance. The ability to print money became a curse, not a blessing. In the end, the fall of a reserve currency empire is not caused by a single event, but by a series of choices that compound over time—choices to delay reform, to placate voters, to protect entrenched interests, and to ignore reality. When debt grows faster than income, when spending outpaces production, and when confidence is replaced by fear, decline becomes irreversible. The final years are marked by division, desperation, and a sense that the future has slipped away.

Chapter 20

Last Fortress

Tariffs, at their core, are a policy tool—a lever that governments pull to intervene in the natural flow of international trade. Their purpose may be to raise revenue, protect domestic industries, or influence trade balances. But beneath the technical façade of tariffs lies a fundamental strategic divergence. On one side are tariffs implemented as part of a broader developmental agenda, aimed at nurturing infant industries toward global competitiveness. On the other are tariffs that serve primarily as defensive walls to shield declining or structurally uncompetitive sectors from global forces. The key difference between these two approaches often comes down to the question of labor cost structures and whether an industry is ascending or descending in the arc of economic relevance. The export-oriented model of tariff policy emerges in economies where the state identifies promising industries that, while not yet competitive on the world stage, possess the potential to become globally viable. These industries often benefit from access to abundant cheap labor, which allows them to produce at lower marginal costs, even when the industries themselves lack scale or technological maturity. In this scenario, tariffs function not as permanent barricades, but as temporary scaffolding—support structures designed to give young industries the breathing room they need to develop productivity, technological know-how, and economies of scale.

This model has been best exemplified in the East Asian miracle economies—South Korea, Taiwan, and to an extent, China. In the 1960s and 70s, South Korea imposed selective tariffs and quotas on imported goods while simultaneously channeling subsidies, credit, and infrastructural support into domestic heavy industries, shipbuilding, and electronics. Importantly, these protections were not open-ended; they were linked to performance metrics. Firms that failed to meet export targets lost their subsidies or credit access. In this way, South Korea avoided the trap of long-term inefficiency, ensuring that protectionism did not devolve into complacency. What powered this model, beyond smart governance, was a vast pool of underemployed, relatively educated labor. Korean workers, paid far less than their Western counterparts, made it possible for domestic producers to compete globally once basic scale and quality thresholds were reached. China's trajectory shares similar contours. In the early reform era, beginning in 1978, Deng Xiaoping's government maintained tariffs and restrictions on key sectors but simultaneously liberalized Special Economic Zones, where export-led growth was turbocharged by cheap labor, currency controls, and tax incentives. Tariffs in this context were part of a transition strategy: they cushioned domestic firms from foreign competition while giving the economy time to reallocate labor from agriculture to light manufacturing. As Chinese firms matured, many began outcompeting Western firms not simply on price, but on speed, flexibility, and increasingly, innovation. Again, the foundation of cheap and plentiful labor was indispensable—it made the protective period cost-effective and paved the way for global integration.

In contrast, the defensive model of tariff protection—often seen in advanced or stagnating economies—is rooted less in long-term competitiveness than in short-term job preservation. Here, tariffs act not as scaffolding, but as life-support systems for industries that are no longer globally viable. These sectors tend to be labor-expensive, structurally inefficient, and capital-intensive. They suffer not from youth or inexperience, but from age, rigidity, and a chronic inability to compete without artificial protection. A classic example of this model can be seen in post-war Western Europe, particularly in the steel and textile industries of the UK and France in the 1970s and 80s. As global competition intensified, particularly from Asia, these industries faced declining margins and mounting unemployment. Governments imposed tariffs and quotas to stem the tide of cheap imports, largely from Japan, Korea, and later China. But unlike the East Asian model, there was no long-term plan to enhance productivity or transition workers into new sectors. The protected industries had high production costs due to strong labor unions, aging infrastructure, and entrenched practices. Instead of using the protection window to modernize or retrain the workforce, firms often used the extra margin to maintain the status quo. Over time, this led to further divergence from global standards, as the industries became more dependent on state support.

The U.S. auto industry provides another telling example. In the 1980s, facing intense competition from Japanese automakers, U.S. manufacturers lobbied for and received "voluntary export restraints" and other protective measures. While this temporarily cushioned Detroit from foreign pressure, it did not compel deep reform. Many U.S. firms delayed investment in fuel efficiency and quality improvements. By contrast, Japanese firms, motivated by competition, doubled down on process innovation, lean manufacturing, and customer satisfaction—eventually outpacing their American rivals. Thus, the tariff protection became a drag rather than a launchpad. The difference, again, comes back to labor economics. In the defensive model, domestic industries operate under high wage structures, often institutionalized through union contracts or legacy pension systems. These wage structures, while socially beneficial, render the industries inherently uncompetitive on a global scale, especially when facing competition from countries with lower labor costs and newer capital equipment. As a result, even if tariffs temporarily protect jobs, they cannot reverse the underlying productivity gap. Moreover, the lack of export ambition means there is no pressure to innovate, no incentive to retool, and no urgency to transition into higher-value-added sectors.

These two models also differ in political economy. Developmental tariffs are usually part of technocratic industrial policies crafted by centralized governments with long-term horizons—often authoritarian or quasi-authoritarian regimes with strong planning agencies. In contrast, defensive tariffs often emerge from pluralist democracies under electoral pressure, where political leaders respond to the immediate cries of displaced workers and distressed industries. The protective impulse, while understandable, tends to favor short-term political gain over structural reform. There's also a difference in institutional feedback loops. In the export-oriented model, success is measured by an industry's ability to compete internationally. Firms that fail to meet benchmarks are cut off from support. In the defensive model, success is measured by the ability to preserve jobs and votes, often leading to lobbying capture and policy inertia. The more the state intervenes to keep an industry alive, the less incentive the industry has to become self-sufficient.

Chapter 21

The Fall

All empires, no matter how vast or powerful, are ultimately subject to the laws of history and economics. There is a natural cycle to imperial rise and fall, shaped not only by military conquests and economic might but by something more subtle—trust. At the height of an empire's strength, its currency becomes a symbol of stability, of value, of a global consensus that this nation will honor its obligations. The reserve currency is not just a financial instrument; it is the final vote of confidence from the world. But when that trust begins to erode, and the internal contradictions of the system start to strain, the final act of the imperial cycle begins. This closing chapter typically ends in one of two ways: through the devastation of war or the slow agony of hyperinflation. The first path—war—is often triggered by geopolitical shifts. As the old empire weakens, new powers rise. These rising states are usually driven by a combination of economic ambition, national pride, and a desire for independence from the financial rules of the current hegemon. They see the dominant empire's privileges as unfair, its control over global finance as exploitative, and its moral authority as hollow. As the dominant power declines, it becomes more defensive. It resists change, clings to old advantages, and begins to treat rising powers not as partners but as threats.

This creates friction. Trade disputes escalate. Proxy conflicts emerge. The competition extends beyond economics into currency systems, technological ecosystems, and even cultural influence. The reserve currency, once neutral, becomes political. Sanctions, asset seizures, and financial exclusions are weaponized. In response, rival powers begin creating alternatives—new payment systems, new alliances, new ways to trade without relying on the dominant currency. Trust in the old system continues to fade, especially among nations that have seen how easily their access to global markets can be cut off. Eventually, one of two outcomes occurs. Either the dominant power cedes influence peacefully, or it attempts to defend its position by force. If it chooses the latter, war becomes likely—not necessarily through a single decision but through a series of escalations. Conflicts may begin over strategic resources, shipping routes, or diplomatic incidents. Each side believes the other will back down. But in a world already straining under economic pressure, political instability, and deep mistrust, miscalculation is easy. Once war begins, it consumes what remains of the old empire's strength. Resources are drained, debt explodes, allies defect, and infrastructure is destroyed. The reserve currency collapses not from choice but from fire.

This is how many reserve currency cycles have ended. Britain's pound sterling, once dominant, lost its position after the enormous costs of two world wars. Before that, the Dutch guilder gave way under the pressures of military overreach and financial exhaustion. War speeds up decline. It forces reality to the surface. The illusion of strength is replaced by the brute arithmetic of destruction. But not every fall ends in flames. There is a second path—one that appears more peaceful but is just as ruinous. When the debt of the empire becomes too great, and when political will to impose discipline has evaporated, the central bank is forced to do the unthinkable: monetize the debt. That is, it begins to buy up government bonds in ever-larger quantities, printing money to fund deficits that can no longer be sustained through taxes or borrowing from the public. This is often justified as necessary for economic stability, but in truth, it is the last lever remaining when all others have failed.

The money supply grows faster than the real economy. Asset prices surge. Real estate, stocks, and luxury goods climb in value, while wages stagnate and necessities become more expensive. The official inflation data may lag, but people feel it. Their purchasing power erodes. Their savings lose value. Their lives become more precarious. As confidence in the currency begins to fall, the pace of money creation accelerates. The government becomes addicted to easy financing. Every new problem—recession, unemployment, social unrest—is met with more spending, more borrowing, more

printing. Foreigners begin to abandon the currency. Demand
for it abroad shrinks. The empire tries to offset this by exporting more currency through imports or financial channels,
but this only increases domestic fragility. Soon, inflation becomes unmanageable. Prices begin to rise not yearly, but
monthly, then weekly. People lose faith not just in the government, but in money itself. They rush to convert their
currency into anything that seems to hold value—gold, foreign currencies, durable goods, even food.

The central bank may attempt to tighten policy, but it is too
late. Raising interest rates would bankrupt the government.
Fiscal tightening would trigger collapse. So the printing continues. Hyperinflation takes hold. This stage is the economic
equivalent of war. It devastates the middle class, wipes out
savings, destroys contracts, and erases decades of trust in
institutions. The social order begins to unravel. Crime increases. Corruption becomes rampant. Political movements
emerge promising salvation, often turning to authoritarian-
ism. In the final phase, the reserve currency loses its status.
New financial centers emerge. The world moves on. And the
empire, now hollowed out, is forced to rebuild on far less fa-
vorable terms. What makes this outcome particularly tragic
is that it happens in full view. Economists warn about the
dangers. Historians point to the past. Even the public begins
to feel the unease. But because the alternative—discipline,
austerity, painful reform—is politically impossible, the cycle
runs its course. There is no escape except through collapse
and reinvention.

Whether through war or hyperinflation, the result is the same. The empire loses its reserve currency status. Its influence fades. Its ability to shape the world diminishes. It becomes just another nation, bound by the same rules as everyone else. This is not necessarily the end of that country, but it is the end of an era. The privilege of issuing the world's money is gone. Trust, once broken, is hard to earn again. And so the cycle ends where it began—with trust. The currency that once commanded the world's confidence no longer does. The power that once shaped global institutions now struggles to govern its own people. The empire, having consumed its future for the illusion of permanence, must face a new reality. And somewhere else in the world, a new power begins to rise—one that saves, builds, produces, and earns the trust of others. The ring has passed, and the world moves on.

We Hope You Enjoyed This Book

Here at Stone Ridge, we gathered a group of people who truly care about the work they deliver. Our goal is not profit, but joy—your joy. Nothing makes us happier than hearing your feedback.

Scan to review the book.

What Will You Read Next?

Our editors carefully review each submission to ensure it meets our standards and is worth your time. If you'd like to discover more books like this one, consider signing up for our newsletter to stay informed about our latest releases. We don't flood your inbox with junk, promise!

Scan to sign up to our newsletter.

About the Author

Dr. Tirdad Aryan is an Iranian-born economist and investor who immigrated to the United States to pursue graduate studies. He earned his Ph.D. in Mechanical Engineering from Northwestern University. Following his doctorate, Dr. Aryan joined the Kellogg School of Management as a researcher, focusing on the effects of sentiment and behavioral factors on equity pricing. Dr. Aryan began his investing career in commodity futures before transitioning to equity and index trading, where he developed quantitative and sentiment-driven strategies. He co-founded BlockHouse Financial, an investment and research firm dedicated to applying behavioral finance principles and macroeconomic insights to modern portfolio management. He currently serves as the firm's Chief Investment Officer.

www.ingramcontent.com/pod-product-compliance
Lightning Source LLC
Chambersburg PA
CBHW060043210326
41520CB00009B/1244